M000248474

# SUPERNATURAL

**EDITED BY
LYNN ZUBERNIS
AND KATHERINE LARSEN**

Credits

First Published in the UK in 2014 by Intellect Books,
The Mill, Parnall Road, Fishponds, Bristol, BS16 3JG, UK

First Published in the USA in 2014 by Intellect Books,
The University of Chicago Press, 1427 E. 60th Street,
Chicago, IL 60637, USA

Copyright © 2014 Intellect Ltd

Editors: Lynn Zubernis and Katherine Larsen

Series Editor and Design: Gabriel Solomons

Typesetting: Stephanie Sarlos

Copy Editor: Emma Rhys

A Catalogue record for this book is available from
the British Library

**Fan Phenomena Series**
ISSN: 2051-4468
eISSN: 2051-4476

**Fan Phenomena: Supernatural**
ISBN: 978-1-78320-203-4
eISBN: 978-1-78320-327-7 / 978-1-78320-328-4

Printed and bound by
Bell & Bain Limited, Glasgow

 intellect

# FAN PHENOMENA

# SUPERNATURAL

*Supernatural* premiered on September 14, 2005 on what was then called the WB Network. Creator Eric Kripke was inspired by Jack Kerouac's *On The Road*, putting his heroes, brothers Sam and Dean Winchester, in a big black '67 Impala and sending them in search of the urban legends that fascinated him. The series attracted a passionate fan base from the start and was described as a 'cultural attractor' that tapped into the zeitgeist of the moment, reflecting global fears of terrorism with its themes of fighting unseen evil. The chemistry between the lead actors, Jared Padalecki and Jensen Ackles, contributed to the show's initial success, and *Supernatural* found its niche when it combined demon-hunting adventures with a powerful relationship drama that explored the intense, complicated bond between the brothers. *Supernatural* is as much a story of familial ties, love, and loyalty as it is of 'saving people, hunting things'.

*Fan Phenomena: Supernatural* is the first book of its kind to explore the ongoing fascination and passion for a show that developed a relationship with fans through eight seasons and continues to have an impact on fan culture to the present day. Essays here explore the rich dynamic that has developed between producers (actors, writers, directors, the show creator, and showrunners) through online interactions on Twitter and Facebook, face-to-face exchanges at conventions, and representations of fandom in canon, such as fourth wall breaking and meta episodes. Contributors also explore gender and sexuality in the show and in fanart; the visual dynamics, cinematography, and symbolism in the episodes as well as the fan videos they inspire; and the culture of influence, learning, and teaching in the series.

**Lynn Zubernis** is a licensed psychologist and an assistant professor at West Chester University. She is the associate editor of the *Journal of Fandom Studies* and recently co-edited *Fan Culture: Theory*. **Katherine Larsen** earned a doctorate in early modern British literature at the University of Maryland, College Park, and currently teaches courses on fame, celebrity, and fandom in the University Writing Program at George Washington University in Washington D.C.

ISBN 978-1-78320-203-4

9 781783 202034

ISBN: 978-1-78320-203-4 / eISBN: 978-1-78320-327-7 & 978-1-78320-328-4
www.intellectbooks.com

# Contents

# Acknowledgements

*Supernatural* is widely referred to within the fandom as "the Little Show That Could," a reflection of its modest beginnings on the now-defunct WB Network, followed by its broadcast on the relatively obscure The CW, and its constant fight against cancellation for its first few seasons. Over the past nine years, we've met countless fans who say that *Supernatural* changed their lives – or even saved their lives. The Show inspires great passion, loyalty, creativity and emotional intensity, all of which contributors to this volume explore. The passion of *Supernatural*'s fans is what kept the Show on the air, from postcard campaigns to Twitter trends, to online voting for TV Guide's first Fan Favorite cover to multiple People's Choice Awards. *Supernatural* is a fan phenomenon in every sense of the word – and it has managed to gain this status while still on the air. Currently in its ninth season, the Little Show That Could still is.

We could not write a volume on *Supernatural* without thanking Eric Kripke, who created the show and was its showrunner for the first five years. Eric's own passion for the show inspired tremendous love and loyalty among the cast and crew, many of whom have been working on the show since the beginning. The talent, creativity and imagination that the cast and crew bring to the show are what brings *Supernatural* to life week after week, from the chemistry between the lead actors to the beauty of the cinematography to the special effects that have led some to describe the look of the show as more like a 42 minute feature film. We're grateful to the cast and crew for each of their unique contributions to *Supernatural*, and for their support of this project.

Finally, we're grateful to our wonderful group of contributors, who wrote about their passion for *Supernatural* from diverse points of view. Some are fans, some are academics, some are actors or crew members on the show. Each contributed his or her unique perspective on the show we've all fallen in love with. Thanks too to Intellect for creating the Fan Phenomena series, and to Gabriel Solomons for believing a show still airing could be a fan phenomenon and then shepherding this volume through.

This is for you, SPN Family. May the Little Show That Could keep right on going!

**Lynn Zubernis and Katherine Larsen**

# Introduction
# Lynn Zubernis and Katherine Larsen

→ *Supernatural* (Eric Kripke, WB/CW Network, 2005–) premiered on 14 September 2005 on what was then called the WB Network. Creator Eric Kripke was inspired by Kerouac's *On The Road* (1957), putting his heroes, brothers Sam and Dean Winchester, in a big black '67 Impala and sending them in search of the urban legends that fascinated him. The series attracted a passionate fan base from the start, with Henry Jenkins describing it in 2007 as a 'cultural attractor' which tapped into the zeitgeist of the moment, reflecting global fears of terrorism with its themes of fighting unseen evil.

The chemistry between the lead actors, Jared Padalecki and Jensen Ackles, contributed to the show's initial success, and *Supernatural* found its niche when it combined demon-hunting adventures with a powerful relationship drama that explored the intense, complicated bond between the brothers. *Supernatural* is as much a story of familial ties, love and loyalty, as it is of 'saving people, hunting things' (the series' unofficial tagline).

From its inception, interaction with fans was encouraged; the studio set up a recording during the first few episodes so that when fans called Dean Winchester's cellphone, they would hear actor Jensen Ackles leaving the message they had heard on the show. The show has furthered its 'reciprocal relationship' with fans through eight seasons of dialogue, illustrating what Jenkins (2006, p. 243) has called the paradigm shift of 'convergence culture', with top-down communication from The Powers That Be giving way to a more complex increasingly bottom-up participatory culture.

In *Fandom at the Crossroads* (2012) Eric Kripke expresses his appreciation for the level of fan participation and investment in *Supernatural*, viewing fanworks and interaction as an indication that the fictional universe he created is a place where fans love to play.

I take it as a compliment as far as the fanfiction between the characters, because what we set out in the beginning to obtain is a really self-contained universe in which fans can come and go, and the rules and progressions are consistent. So just as in all other good universes, you can find new ways to expand and explore other corners of that universe [...] and the fact that the fans are actually doing that is a good sign. I love it and I welcome it. I wanted to create a universe where we welcome others to come and play, and it means we're developing a fresh universe successfully. (p. 214)

Despite its relatively small size, there is no doubt that *Supernatural* (known to fans as *SPN*) is now one of the most active fandoms in the world. The show won the first 'fan favourite' cover of *TV Guide* and numerous People's Choice Awards for favourite network drama and sci-fi show. By the beginning of 2013, there had been 56 *Supernatural* conventions held in the United States, Canada, Italy, Brazil, United Kingdom, Spain, Germany, France and Australia. Fans from nearly 200 counties have logged onto the *Supernatural* Wiki (www.supernaturalwiki.com), an online resource of all things *SPN*.

*Supernatural* is widely referred to, by fans, cast and crew, as 'the little show that could', achieving fan phenomenon status with little help from the network. But what is it about a film, book or television show that creates the level of passion, devotion and loyalty which qualify it as such? In these chapters, we explore the evolution of *Supernatural* and its fandom to answer that question. The contributors hold multiple perspectives – they are fans, academics, cast and crew. Each chapter uses the writer's unique lens to illuminate the ways in which *Supernatural* has become a fan phenomenon – by inspir-

## Introduction
Lynn Zubernis and Katherine Larsen

*Figure 1: Jared Padalecki and Jensen Ackles with Supernatural's People's Choice Award for Favorite Fan Following (photo by Christopher Schmelke)*

ing identification, emotional expression and passion; as a catalyst for individual and social change; by facilitating the creation of close bonds of community and collaboration; and by inspiring the teaching of another generation of creators, consumers and fans.

One of the yardsticks by which we pronounce a film, book or television show a 'fan phenomenon' is its incorporation into the ways in which we pass knowledge on to the next generation of media consumers, critics and scholars. The narrative complexity of the *Supernatural* 'text' has led to its incorporation in both high school and college curricula. Paul Booth, in his chapter 'Teaching through *Supernatural*: Using *SPN* in the College Classroom', describes how he uses *SPN* in a course on media and cultural studies. Incorporating *Supernatural* episodes allows an exploration of a wide range of topics, including gender roles, objectification, and violence, through psychological and sociological lenses. The show also provides a way to examine the construction of ideology and religion, and postmodern elements such as self-referentiality (in its trademark meta episodes). It is this complexity that has drawn so many viewers more deeply into the show and thus more deeply into fandom.

Bridget Kies, in 'The Monstrous Male Body', picks up on several of the themes that Booth highlights in his teaching. The fascination with monsters and the monstrous has been a touchstone of the series from its inception, and the bodies of main characters Sam, Dean and Castiel are frequently monstrous through possession. While the characters clearly experience this as traumatic, the fans take pleasure in the objectification of the boys' bodies, monstrous or not – something the show does not discourage with its extreme close-ups, shirtless scenes and frequent hurt/comfort narratives. Sam, when possessed by the demon Meg, was violent and disturbing; fans also found 'Meg!Sam' incredibly hot. Kies explores themes of sexuality, gender, violence and objectification in the show itself, as well as the ways fans interpret those themes and make them their own.

Lisa Macklem explores in more depth another of the themes which Booth uses in his teaching – the self-referentiality of *Supernatural*. In her chapter, 'I See What You Did There: *SPN* and the Fourth Wall', Macklem points out that the ways in which viewers interact with television have changed substantially in the last decade. *Supernatural* has been at the forefront of that change. The show has repeatedly broken the fourth wall, lampooning itself and its fandom in a string of meta episodes that incorporate its knowledge of fan activities into the canon of the series itself. Cast and crew and even the writers interact directly with fans over social media and at fan conventions. Macklem emphasizes the ability of both sides to make fun of each other, drawing a parallel to the way a family interacts.

In the next chapter, Jules Wilkinson, the administrator of the SuperWiki (the place to go for anything and everything you ever wanted to know about *Supernatural*), celebrates the epic love story of *Supernatural* Fandom and social media. Even the writers, actors and showrunners depend on the SuperWiki to ensure continuity, so it's no surprise that Wilkinson is a thorough and humorous chronicler of *Supernatural*'s history. Wilkinson follows the fandom from a small genre-show following to a global phenomenon, exploring the ways in which the evolution of social media paralleled and facilitated the evolution of *Supernatural* fandom. As fans shared fanworks and built communities on various platforms, the cohesiveness of the *SPN* fandom grew. From the start, the fandom has been international, with fans from every corner of the globe coming together in cyberspace and at fan conventions.

Mary Frances Casper examines more closely the identity of the *Supernatural* fandom as 'family', a word the fans themselves have chosen to characterize their diverse global community, in her chapter 'Family Don't End with Blood: Building the *Supernatural* Family'. Casper traces the creation of communal myths over time, which indicate belonging, express family identity and evoke shared history, thus creating a family narrative that comes to exist independent of the show which originally inspired it. The People's Choice Awards in 2013 even adopted the name '*SPN* Family' for *Supernatural* fandom in its contest for 'Favourite TV Fan Following'. And yes, we won.

The power of the *Supernatural* fandom is often expressed as social activism, a theme that Mary F. Dominiak explores in the next chapter, '*Supernatural*: Making a Difference is the Meaning of Life'. Dominiak describes how *Supernatural* fans have taken the show's motto 'saving people, hunting things – the family business' to heart, translating the challenge of saving people to social activism and helping others. The Winchester brothers' emphasis on family is taken by fans to promote the value of caring for others as family. For *Supernatural* fans, banding together to fight disease, homelessness, disaster and abuse is analogous to hunters fighting demons, ghosts and monsters. The show's meta episodes depict fanboys and fangirls rising to the occasion to literally save the day, suggesting that we can all make a difference.

Several actors, most notably Misha Collins with his Random Acts charity, have been an organizing force behind *Supernatural* fans coming together for social change. Collins, who portrays the angel Castiel on *Supernatural*, expands on Dominiak's thoughts on the fandom impulse for social change by providing his unique perspective on that impulse. Fans often talk about being 'blindsided' by *Supernatural* and sucked into the wild ride of *SPN* fandom; Collins feels the same about the fandom. He analyses his own

**Introduction**
Lynn Zubernis and Katherine Larsen

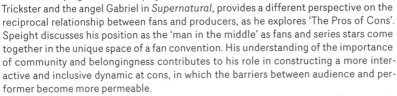

*Figure 2: "We have each other's backs" - Jared and Jensen, and the SPN family (photo by Karen Cooke)*

evolution as a reluctant 'celebrity', struggling with defining boundaries and making sense of the sudden and unexpected adoration. His eventual understanding of the creative potential in fandom, and his realization that he shared with fans the impulse toward social change, resulted in the establishment of Random Acts.

Richard Speight, Jr., who played The Trickster and the angel Gabriel in *Supernatural*, provides a different perspective on the reciprocal relationship between fans and producers, as he explores 'The Pros of Cons'. Speight discusses his position as the 'man in the middle' as fans and series stars come together in the unique space of a fan convention. His understanding of the importance of community and belongingness contributes to his role in constructing a more interactive and inclusive dynamic at cons, in which the barriers between audience and performer become more permeable.

*Supernatural* fans love the show for many reasons, including its excellence in cinematography and visual appeal. There are entire online communities devoted to the show's distinctive 'look', and fans analyse the set decoration, production, lighting and filming techniques closely, looking for the same sort of subtextual meaning that they find in dialogue, characterization and plot. Director of photography Serge Ladouceur offers his perspective on making *Supernatural* visually powerful. Once again, the theme of family and sense of cohesion that mark the fandom come through in Serge's emphasis on collaboration as the core of *Supernatural*'s success.

The visual appeal of *Supernatural* inspires a wide variety of fanworks, from fanart to fan videos. Popular vidder Sarah House, known within the *Supernatural* fandom as Ash48, offers insights into how the show inspires her creativity and what it means to her to be a *Supernatural* fan. Like all the contributors to this volume, Sarah recognizes the richly layered complexity of the show, and the sense of community created by the shared search for meaning, as the ingredients of a true fan phenomenon. ●

~~~~~~~~

**GO FURTHER**

**Books**

Lynn Zubernis and Katherine Larsen
*Fandom at the Crossroads: Celebration, Shame and Fan/Producer Relationships*
(Newcastle upon Tyne, UK: Cambridge Scholars Publishing, 2012)

Jack Kerouac
*On The Road*: 50th Anniversary Edition
(New York: Viking Press, 1957)

Henry Jenkins
*Convergence Culture*
(New York: NYUP, 2006)

**Film/Television**

*Supernatural*, Eric Kripke, creator (Los Angeles: Warner Brothers, 2005–)

**Online**

'Supernatural: First Impressions'
Henry Jenkins
*Confessions of an Aca-Fan*. 15 January 2007, http://henryjenkins.org/2007/01/super-natural.html.

'People's Choice Awards: 2013 Winners: Favorite TV Fan Following: SPNFamily, Super-natural'. People's Choice, 9 January 2013 http://www.peopleschoice.com/pca/awards/nominees/.

Chapter
1

# Teaching Through *Supernatural*: Using *SPN* in the College Classroom

Paul Booth

→ **Then …**
Like on most Friday nights, my wife and I walked our dogs, ordered the sushi, and at 8 p.m. tuned to the CW to catch the latest episode of *Supernatural*. As was my habit, I had my laptop open while the show was airing (I know, sacrilegious for a fan, but I think my students had an assignment due that night). And while I wasn't really playing with the computer, I did have the screen up on my latest project: (re)designing the syllabus for MCS 271: Media and Cultural Studies …

**Now …**
… It felt as if Castiel Himself led me to see the connection between the show that was airing and the syllabus on my laptop. Although I'd been looking for a way to 'shake up' the foundation of our College's required cultural studies course, I hadn't had a great deal of success. But thanks to that moment of concomitant viewing – that moment of divine intervention – I was able to see how *Supernatural* could be integrated into each lesson taught in that class. In the past, I have included 45-minute screenings of television shows and short films to illustrate the different cultural studies methods of analysing media. Most recently, I used relevant episodes of *Supernatural* that fit into the schema of the class. I hoped this would allow me to use my own fandom for *SPN* as a way of demonstrating to the students how different theories of the media worked together. And, *Supernatural* not only succeeded, but excelled at this goal. In this chapter, I'll be discussing the ways that I integrated episodes of *Supernatural* in my Media and Cultural Studies course. I'll begin by summarizing the structure and teaching emphasis in the class itself. Next, I'll offer some lesson plans to more fully articulate the multiple interpretations of *Supernatural*. Finally, I'll look at the ways students seemed to respond positively to *Supernatural*.

**'Nightmare': Teaching cultural studies**
The course objectives for MCS 271 ask that at the end of the course, students be able to:

1. Write clearly and cogently about theories of the media;
2. Demonstrate the application of media theories to media texts; and
3. Criticize contemporary media texts through the use of theories.

Using *Supernatural* helped reach these objectives. It also reached, however, a higher-level objective that I didn't necessarily intend. When I talk about 'levels of objectives', I'm referring to Benjamin Bloom's *Taxonomy of Learning Objectives* (1984), which ranks the levels at which different skills are necessary for learning. For example, the first level is 'knowledge', which asks students to know and repeat back important information. As the levels increase, the difficulty of attaining that level rises. The next skill, 'comprehension', requires knowledge as well as critical thinking. The other levels – 'application', 'analysis', 'evaluation', and finally 'creation' – come with more intense styles of learning. Because MCS 271 is an introductory course, I aim for the simpler levels: knowledge, comprehension and application.
The first time I taught the course, I found that students were able to approach the *application* stage. They could view each text and apply the theory we were learning to it. The second time I taught the course – the *SPN* time – I found that students were able to reach the *analysis* stage – a more advanced level. Because we watched episodes from one television show instead of multiple texts, students were able to make connections

**Teaching Trough *Supernatural: SPN* in the College Classroom**
Paul Booth

between the different media theories. I believe this is partly because of what TV scholar Jason Mittell would call the 'narrative complexity' of *Supernatural* – that is, the way the show uses both stand-alone episodes as well as a longer narrative arc to tell multiple stories. Students understood the connections between episodes even if they didn't follow the whole narrative because they at least knew that there was supposed to be an overarching story.

I break the course into ten topics, each of which revolves around issues in cultural studies. Given the audience of the class, freshmen and sophomores, I aim for breadth rather than depth. The ten topics are:

1. The Subject (and Study) of Culture
2. Semiotics and Structuralism
3. Ideology and Hegemony
4. Political Economy, Marxism, and the Economics of Culture
5. Representation and Race
6. Psychoanalysis and Gender Studies
7. Reception Studies and Fandom
8. Postmodernism and Contemporary Philosophy
9. Genre Studies
10. Digital Culture

When I first taught MCS 271, I used multiple 'classic' texts to illustrate the topics. None of these classic texts related to one another. In class, however, I found that students were generally able to make comparisons between the *theory* and the *text* for that particular topic, but didn't seem able to make these larger connections between the theories themselves. When I added *Supernatural*, as the following section demonstrates, students were better able to achieve higher learning objectives.

### 'Devil's trap: Introducing *Supernatural* to cultural studies (and vice versa)

Generally in class I take students (via discussion) through the different types of 'meaning' to be found in media texts, as described by the classic film textbook *Making Meaning* (1991) by David Bordwell. For Bordwell, there are four ways to find meaning in a text. The first, the 'referential', is the most obvious: the basic plot. In class, I ask students to identify what happened on-screen, how the characters reacted to this and what the results of that were. When we explore the second way to find meaning, the 'explicit', I ask them to describe the *moral* of the text. This is usually stated in the show as the lesson to be learned.

The class tends to have more difficulty with the third level of meaning, the 'implicit', as it only arrives through careful consideration of what the producers of the media text implied by the moral. This isn't something stated in the show, but rather a more general feeling or theme. Finally, I ask students to explore the 'symptomatic' meaning, which examines the ideology that shaped the text, and then what we can learn through critical reflection.

To enable this fourth meaning, I give students two readings for each class. The first is a 'theory' reading from the textbooks I use, Professor Greg Smith's *What Media Classes Really Want to Discuss* (2010) and Arthur Asa Berger's *Media Analysis Techniques* (2011). The theory reading explains the topic for the day. The second reading tends to be an example of that type of theory when put in use. I then try to pair each class with a specific episode of *SPN* that demonstrates that particular theme, as illustrated in Table 1. Although in this chapter I don't have space to discuss all ten classes, I will go into detail with four of them: The Study of Culture, Ideology, Psychoanalysis, and Postmodernism.

| Class | Subject | Episode | Theory Readings | Show Rationale |
|-------|---------|---------|-----------------|----------------|
| 01 | The Subject (and Study) of Culture | 'Pilot' (Season 1, Episode1) | Smith, Chapter 1, 'Why you should analyse film and television' | Introduce characters, narrative, themes |
| 02 | Semiotics and Structuralism | 'The Usual Suspects' (Season 2, Episode 7) | Berger, Chapter 1, 'Semiotic analysis' (I pair this with a short piece by Lisa Coulthard about the symbolism of TV show title sequences) | Use of language and symbols to solve clues |
| 03 | Ideology and Hegemony | 'Hammer of the Gods' (Season 5, Episode 19) | Smith, Chapter 2, 'What is realism, anyway?' | Illustration of the hierarchy of religions |
| 04 | Political Economy, Marxism, Economics | 'Wishful Thinking' (Season 4, Episode 8) | Berger, Chapter 2, 'Marxist analysis' | Illustration of moral, use of economics in show |

**Teaching Trough *Supernatural: SPN* in the College Classroom**
Paul Booth

| 05 | Representation and Race | 'Family Matters' (Season 6, Episode 5) (clips of 'Route 666' [Season 1, Episode 13]) | Smith, Chapter 6, 'Role models and stereotypes: an introduction to the "Other"' (I pair this with Peg McIntosh's 'Unpacking the Invisible Knapsack') | Discussion of the representation of the African alpha vampire and of race in 'Route 666' paired with a discussion of the Winchesters' White Privilege |
|---|---|---|---|---|
| 06 | Psychoanalysis and Gender Studies | 'Dead Man's Blood' (Season 1, Episode 20) | Berger, Chapter 3, 'Psychoanalytic criticism' | Illustration of the male gaze |
| 07 | Reception Studies and Fandom | 'The Real Ghostbusters' (Season 5, Episode 9) | Smith, Chapter 3, 'How do we identify with characters?' | Discussion of how fandom and fan communities are depicted in the show, and how that is or is not reflective of students' own stereotypes |
| 08 | Postmodernism and Contemporary Philosophy | 'The French Mistake' (Season 6, Episode 15) | Berger, Chapter 4, 'Sociological analysis' Smith, Chapter 8, 'What is interactivity?' (I pair this with Peter Barry's 'Postmodernism' chapter) | Illustration of self-reflexive and self-parodic text |
| 09 | Genre Studies | 'Changing Channels' (Season 5, Episode 8) | Smith, Chapter 4, 'Genre shmenre' | Discussion of the multiple representations of genre in this episode and how viewers know what genre it is from the semantic, syntactic and pragmatic signs |
| 10 | Digital Culture | 'Hollywood Babylon' (Season 2, Episode 18) | Berger, Chapter 9, 'Video games: A new art form' and Chapter 10, 'Cell phones, social media, and the problem of identity' | Illustration of cellular technology to defeat ghosts and the way video game aesthetics have crept into the show |

## The study of culture

The first class introduces students to cultural studies, which I define as the analysis of critical thinking about the way humans construct their existence in the world. By showing the students 'Pilot' for the Subject (and Study) of Culture, I meet two goals. The first is introducing the characters, narrative and themes of *Supernatural* in the way the producers intended. The second is letting the students learn about the way culture is constructed through a relatively easy-to-read episode. The first episode doesn't rely on viewers' inherent knowledge about the show and includes some pretty simple themes throughout. For example, a common analysis in media studies is to look at the representation of women in the media (is it stereotypical? Do they fulfill traditional gender roles?). In the case of *Supernatural*, there is a strong emphasis in the first episode on linking Sam and Dean's mother to Sam's girlfriend. We can see this in the representations of the death of Sam and Dean's mother (Figure 1) with the death of Sam's girlfriend (Figure 2). By linking these two characters *visually*, the show links them *thematical-*

*Figure 3: 'Hammer of the Gods'*

*ly* – that is, it is drawing a connection between *motherhood* and *femininity*. It's a rather obvious visual trick in the show, and even without much experience in cultural studies, my students have been able to identify it pretty easily.

We engage in other discussions of *theme* in this first class, including the show's violence and the way it links familial bonds, vengeance, and the educational system – Dean is wiser because he is 'street smart'; despite his schooling, Sam has a lot to learn about the 'real world' – something my students enjoyed noticing. I intend this first class to introduce not only the show, but also the way scholars can investigate the media.

The class on Ideology, coming third in the schedule, is really the first time the class explores an unfamiliar and confusing topic. I define ideology as the way our cultural belief systems are constructed by factors all around us: the media, our families, politicians, even the educational system. My goal for the class is that students learn that what we believe to be a *natural way of thinking* is usually constructed by others for us to believe. Using the episode 'Hammer of the Gods' to illustrate ideology works well because it offers a chance for students to talk about value systems without delving into their own personal beliefs.

I talk with the students about the representation of the different religions on-screen. The conversation generally turns to how some are violent, others are animalistic, and some are seen as scheming. This, I say, is explicit in the show. We discuss how this represents religion in general and the underlying meaning of religion in this context. The point of our discussion, though, arrives when we talk about the *implicit* depiction of the religions. Which religion, I ask, is 'in charge'? Which are subordinate to it (Figure 3)?

When the class identifies Christianity as the major religion, I ask why the producers would have done this. The class seems to see this as an automatic choice – a decision that required no thought because the producers are working in a Judeo-Christian environment for a largely Judeo-Christian audience. Putting Odin as the 'head' of the religions wouldn't have made sense given the underlying ideological structure of the culture in which the episode appeared. This then offers a useful entrance into talking about how some ideas became naturalized and how others then become alien to us. I can then usually transition smoothly into the formation of false choice (are these the only religions?) and interpellation – how the media address viewers.

## Psychoanalysis

For the topic of Psychoanalysis, I use the episode 'Dead Man's Blood'. In that episode, the Winchesters come across a nest of vampires who are trying to get their claws on John's magical Colt. One scene in particular stands out in class: one (female) vampire

Figure 4 'Dead Man's Blood'

Figure 5: 'Dead Man's Blood'

erotically 'turns' a (female) human into a vampire (Figure 4) for the pleasure of her (male) vampire companion (Figure 5). The audience watches the male watching the women.

This echoes precisely the three 'looks' of the cinema, as introduced by film scholar Laura Mulvey. For Mulvey, the three 'looks' of the cinema – the camera at the actors, the men on-screen and the audience at the characters – are all shaped by sexism. That is, all three objectify women. This scene from 'Dead Man's Blood' perfectly fits all three looks (in truth, the same could be said in reverse: Sam and Dean are often objectified as well in the show!).

Furthermore, throughout the episode, the three Winchester men – Sam, Dean and John – all vie for power to see who will be in charge of their attack. Dean acts impulsively, doing what he feels best. Sam acts rationally, trying to 'out-think' the others. John tries to mediate between the two of them. After reading through the section of the textbook on Freud's discussion of the id, ego and superego in human consciousness, the class quite easily identifies each Winchester with one of these characteristics. Our discussion allows us to explore how Freud's categories can be seen across different episodes as well – there's almost always an impulsive character (the id), a rational character (the superego), and a character that mediates (the ego). This happens in most media texts. In this way, I can use the episode to focus class discussion more specifically on both the way women are objectified by the media and on the way the media represents conflict through Freud's psychoanalysis.

### Postmodernism

I follow a similar trajectory through the analysis of Postmodernism and 'The French Mistake'. Postmodernism is a type of analysis that relies on (among other things) self-referentiality to highlight the 'constructed' nature of the media. This episode tells of the brothers' trip into a parallel dimension where Sam and Dean Winchester are characters on a television show played by the actors Jared Padalecki and Jensen Ackles. Sam

**Teaching Trough *Supernatural: SPN* in the College Classroom**
Paul Booth

*Figure 6: 'The French Mistake'*

and Dean have to pretend to be these doppelgängers in order to get home. The self-referentiality of the show continues throughout – the producers share the names of their on-screen counterparts, jokes about the show's low ratings abound, actor Misha Collins portrays himself as a sycophantic wannabe actor, and Dean even finds a '*Supernatural* Magazine' (Figure 6).

Beyond the obvious humour of the episode, there are a number of postmodern elements that make discussing the show in class easy and fun. From philosopher Peter Barry's chapter titled 'Postmodernism', we identify the major characteristics of this philosophical movement, including the fact that there is no inherent truth (what is the 'real' reality in 'The French Mistake'?) and that there has been an increase in the use of 'intertextuality' and 'pastiche' in the media. Both intertextuality and pastiche describe how different styles or genres can be pasted into a piece of media to create a new type of story. I ask students to point out an example of that characteristic from 'The French Mistake', an example from a different episode of *Supernatural*, and an example from something else they've watched. When we discuss, we find as a class how these characteristics manifest throughout contemporary media.

*Supernatural* has proven to be a useful teaching tool in the class. Not only does it offer a unique reference point for each topic, but it also provides a continuing narrative to which my students can comment. Furthermore, because of my own fandom of *Supernatural*, examples of which I am happy to share with the class, the show becomes more meaningful to the students; it has a real presence in their minds because of the excitement I show and the devotion I describe. In the next section, I'll go into a bit more detail about how my students responded to the show.

## 'Something wicked': Teaching with *Supernatural*

Although an imprecise measurement, student course evaluations are useful for at least generating discussion about the ideas and methods of classroom instruction. And in that respect, the evaluations I received for teaching with *Supernatural* were universally positive, in contrast to the course evaluations in the past that were more hesitant in their praise.

Reactions to the class emphasized the usefulness of using this media text over using many. For example, one student wrote that *Supernatural* 'taught me different ways of looking at media and essentially, the world'. Another said that as a media text, the show had 'excellent use of examples for practically every topic covered'. Finally, a third thought that '*Supernatural* is really entertaining too and it helps to see what we learn in class in actuality'. In contrast, evaluations from the previous class included statements like 'The topic of Ideology was definitely interesting, [but] it [...] was the most difficult topic to grasp'. Students in the past seemed to have trouble making the connections and seeing the bigger picture than did students in my *SPN* course.

Other students thought that using *Supernatural* instead of more esoteric (read: older) media texts had a more relevant impact on their learning. For example, one student wrote 'It really gave me insight into media and showed me the power that media has in society'. Another: 'It was very easy to follow along and actually learn the material instead of just memorizing things to spit back at the professor'. Finally, the last comment students left about the class's use of *Supernatural* summed up precisely what I had hoped people would get out of the course: 'This course was most helpful to me in the sense that it provided a new perspective in the way people view media, and how that view can be distorted based on various outside factors'.

Interestingly, there was no blowback from the students or the administration on using a show that is as violent, scary and bloody as *SPN*. Initially, students in the class seemed sceptical of the show merely because it seemed cheesy. 'Why would we screen something from the CW network?' they seemed to think. But I spent a quarter of an hour explaining my rationale for using the show and what I hoped they would glean from it, and there were no complaints afterwards.

Additionally, my students' in-class work noticeably improved from the first time I taught the course to the second. Students participated more, were more engaged, and offered more opinions than in previous years. The class had livelier discussions, students interacted with each other, and I found myself participating in engrossing discussions rather than just asking question after question to a bored classroom.

In sum, *Supernatural* works in class because of my fandom. As a fan of the show, I am energized when I discuss it. I laugh loudly at the funny parts, cry when tragedy strikes, am moved by the brothers' care for one another. I am not just a passive recipient of the text, but rather an active and engaged viewer, who responds to what he sees. When we talk about the show, I share my opinions. The show becomes 'real' to me and to my students as well. After leaving class, my students become better media viewers, better media scholars, and better media fans. ●

**Teaching Trough *Supernatural: SPN* in the College Classroom**
Paul Booth

~~~~~~~~~~

**GO FURTHER**

**Books**

*Media Analysis Techniques*, 4th edn
Arthur Asa Berger
(Thousand Oaks, CA: Sage, 2011)

*What Media Classes Really Want to Discuss*
Greg Smith
(New York: Routledge, 2010)

*Beginning Theory: An Introduction to Literary and Cultural Theory*, 3ʳᵈ edn
Peter Barry
(Manchester, UK: MUP, 2009)

*Making Meaning: Inference and Rhetoric in the Interpretation of Cinema.*
David Bordwell
(Boston, MA: Harvard University Press, 1991)

*Taxonomy of Educational Objectives*
Benjamin Bloom
(Boston, MA: Allyn and Bacon, 1984)

**Extracts/Essays/Articles**

'Narrative complexity in contemporary American television'
Jason Mittell
In *The Velvet Light Trap*. 58:3(2006), pp. 29–40.

'Visual pleasure and narrative cinema'
Laura Mulvey
In *Screen*. 16:3 (1975), pp. 6–18.

**Film/Television**

*Supernatural*, Eric Kripke, creator (Los Angeles: Warner Brothers, 2005–)

'Pilot', David Nutter, dir. *Supernatural* (Los Angeles: Warner Brothers, 2005)

'Hammer of the Gods', Rick Bota, dir. *Supernatural*
(Los Angeles: Warner Brothers, 2010)

'Dead Man's Blood', Tony Wharmby, dir. *Supernatural*
(Los Angeles: Warner Brothers, 2006)

'The French Mistake', Charles Beeson, dir. *Supernatural*
(Los Angeles: Warner Brothers, 2011)

'The Usual Suspects' Mike Rohl, dir. *Supernatural*
(Los Angeles: Warner Brothers, 2006)

'Wishful Thinking' Robert Singer, dir. *Supernatural*
(Los Angeles: Warner Brothers, 2008)

'Family Matters' Guy Bee, dir. *Supernatural* (Los Angeles: Warner Brothers, 2010)

'Route 666' Paul Shapiro, dir. *Supernatural* (Los Angeles: Warner Brothers, 2006)

'The Real Ghostbusters' James L. Conway, dir. *Supernatural*
(Los Angeles: Warner Brothers, 2009)

'Changing Channels' Charles Beeson, dir. *Supernatural*
(Los Angeles: Warner Brothers, 2009)

'Hollywood Babylon' Phil Sgriccia, dir. *Supernatural*
(Los Angeles: Warner Brothers, 2007)

**Online**

'Familiarity breeds desire: Seriality and the televisual title sequence'
Lisa Coulthard
*FlowTV*. 2 July 2010, http://flowtv.org/2010/07/familiarity-breeds-desire/.

*White privilege: Unpacking the invisible knapsack*
Peg McIntosh
1988, http://www.nymbp.org/reference/WhitePrivilege.pdf.

# Chapter
2

# The Monstrous Male Body

## Bridget Kies

→ Brothers Sam and Dean Winchester (Jared Padalecki and Jensen Ackles) of WB/CW's *Supernatural* live in a world where monsters are real, and Sam and Dean's mission is to hunt them – a mission requiring frequent examination of how they define a 'monster'. Over the course of the series, their definition moves from something concrete (not a human), to something with exceptions (it's not a monster if it doesn't kill humans), to the Winchesters themselves. Through stories of demonic possession and insinuations of rape, the series perverts the male body into something monstrous. Although this perversion is something the Winchesters want to stop, fans revel in it season after season.

*Figure 1: A close-up of Sam with injuries from a car accident shows the pleasure and pain of watching the characters suffer, ('In My Time of Dying' [Season 2, Episode 1]).*

Often insinuated as the primary reason many female viewers watch *Supernatural*, the beautiful faces and bodies of Padalecki and Ackles have long been a subject of discussion among fans and scholars.[1] The series objectifies the male body through shower and sex scenes and frequent close-ups of faces. In fanfiction and fanart, Padalecki's/Sam's long hair and Ackles's/Dean's pouty lips are routinely fetishized.

What would seem to be at work, therefore, are two conflicting narratives. Within the series is the story of two brothers whose bodies are frequently rendered monstrous, while outside the series the beauty of the two actors is celebrated by fans. But these two narratives are actually interdependent. Fan/blogger athomemomblog asks a question many fans have contemplated: 'Is it just me or are guys on TV cuter when they're all banged up?' While fans do enjoy turning their gaze on Sam and Dean, they take particular delight in doing so when the brothers' bodies are being abused.[2]

According to Barbara Creed (2005), a man can become monstrous in horror films when he forfeits his phallus and 'attempts to usurp the primary functions of woman, particularly in relation to reproduction, sexuality, and birth' (p. 50). Creed's idea draws

## The Monstrous Male Body
Bridget Kies

*Figure 2: Jo being tortured by Sam, who is being possessed by Meg in 'Born Under a Bad Sign'*

upon Freud's concept of the castration complex, the lifelong fear all men have of losing their penis. Storylines in *Supernatural* depict the castration complex by turning the male body into the monstrous-feminine: as an object for possession, as a virgin or as a womb/mother. Other scholars have discussed the prevalence of torture and hurt/comfort both within the series and its fandom. Rather than concentrating on that aspect of abuse, I will examine the male body-turned-female as a monstrosity the canon seeks to mitigate, even as fans take pleasure in it.

### 'You full-on had a girl inside'[3]
In the series' storyworld, demons, ghosts and angels can all possess human bodies, an experience that is always traumatic for the host. Jimmy Novak describes serving as the host vessel for the angel Castiel as 'being chained to a comet' ('The Rapture' [Season 4, Episode 20]). Equally traumatic is witnessing what the supernatural creature might do with the body while the human has no control. One demon even manages to impregnate a woman it is possessing, causing her to give birth to a human-demon hybrid ('I Believe the Children Are Our Future' [Season 5, Episode 6]).[4] After the demon called Meg is exorcised from a young woman (the real Meg), the woman explains that she had to watch, helpless, as her relationship with her family was destroyed ('Devil's Trap' [Season 1, Episode 22]; 'Are You There God? It's Me, Dean Winchester' [Season 4, Episode 2]).

*Figure 3: Sam and Dean show off their matching tattoos in 'Jus in Bello,' (Season 3, Episode 12)*

As principal players in this supernatural world, the Winchesters are also susceptible to possession. When Sam is possessed by Meg, he steals, smokes, commits a violent murder and nearly rapes Jo, a friend and fellow hunter. Meg!Sam, as he is called in the fandom, also shoots Dean and leaves him for dead, but Dean is ultimately able to capture him and exorcise the demon ('Born Under a Bad Sign' [Season 2, Episode 14]).

It is the scene with Jo that particularly reveals the horror of Sam's possession. In the series' mythology, demons originate as humans. This means they have gender, typically the same as that of the bodies they possess. Meg's possession of Sam reverses the traditional gender dynamic of the male possessing the female body through marriage or sexual penetration. At face value, Meg's treatment of Jo is an attack on a woman (Jo) by a man (Sam), since neither the viewer nor Jo knows Sam is possessed until later. But this is really a double rape: the female demon 'rapes' the human male body through possession, in order to make the human male (nearly) rape a human female.

After Meg is exorcised, Dean teases Sam that he 'full-on had a girl inside'. For Dean, this grotesque victimization threatens Sam's masculinity. In his work on psychoanalysis and the body, Leo Bersani theorizes that for a man '[t]o be penetrated is to abdicate power' (p. 19). Barbara Creed (1993) similarly argues that possession means 'the boundary between self and other has been transgressed. When the subject is invaded by [...] another sex the transgression is even more abject because gender boundaries are violated' (p. 32). When Meg penetrates Sam's body, she renders Sam powerless. In Dean's eyes, being powerless at the hands of a female doubles the insult of possession.

Unlike Sam and Dean, many fans enjoy Sam's possession. This episode continues to be a fan favourite in informal surveys, and fans frequently comment on Meg!Sam's hotness. Also popular are fanfiction stories in which one brother is possessed and rapes or tortures the other. Although Sam's possession only lasted one episode, its legacy persists in these stories, in fanart and in communities devoted to celebrating Meg as a badass.

In order to stave off future possessions, the Winchesters get special matching tattoos. In a 2008 interview with C. P. Cochran, Sera Gamble, then a writer and producer, said, 'I'll be convinced we're truly a cult hit when a fan gets the same tattoo.' Many fans have adopted the tattoo design as a mark of their passion for the show and posted their images to the *Supernatural* Wiki's article on fan tattoos. Perhaps in response to this popularity, the series features a character, significantly also a fan, who happily shows her version of the tattoo to Sam and Dean ('The Monster at the End of This Book' [Season 4, Episode 18]). While the Winchesters choose to tattoo their bodies out of fear of another monstrous possession, this character and the real-life fans she emulates do it as a signifier of pleasure.

The Winchesters' fear of possession also extends to their fated roles as angelic hosts. In the fifth season, they learn the apocalypse will be enacted through their bodies, with Sam serving as the vessel for Lucifer and Dean for the Archangel Michael. To protect them from the angels, Castiel carves sigils into their ribs. Like the anti-possession tattoos, the sigils offer protection but also damage their bodies. Because Castiel carved the sigils without permission, the damage may be seen as a way of branding the Winchesters. This alternate form of possession – ownership – coexists with bodily possession as a monstrosity. After being saved from hell by Castiel at the start of Season 4, Dean discovers a scar in the shape of Castiel's handprint on his shoulder. As Suzette Chan explains, 'the angel handprint [...] indicate[s] who owns him, and how', and this ownership is a threat to Dean's masculinity in that a man should be master of himself. The handprint is not seen in Seasons 6 or 7. Since the canon offers no explanation for what happened, fans devise their own theories. A common belief is that Castiel healed the scar when he healed Dean's other wounds in 'Swan Song' (Season 5, Episode 22); Jensen Ackles has echoed his agreement with this theory at several fan conventions. I

**The Monstrous Male Body**
Bridget Kies

would argue that since Dean thwarts his destiny of enacting the apocalypse, it is fitting the handprint disappears. By exercising his free will, Dean demonstrates that he is not, in fact, heaven's property; this is one of the few times the Winchesters are able to reassert claim to their bodies.

*Figure 4: Dean is branded by Castiel in 'Lazarus Rising' (Season 4, Episode 1)*

### 'Brother, I have been rehymenated, and the dude will not abide'⁵

Dean expresses what little power he has over his body through sex, in a series of one-night stands and endless flirtation. Perhaps the most extreme case of this is his knee-jerk reaction to his impending death: he engages in a three-way with twins while Sam waits for him in the car ('The Magnificent Seven' [Season 3, Episode 1]). Popular culture has long depicted scenarios of the sexually active man as stud and, conversely, the male virgin as loser. Jonathan A. Allan reminds us that while female virginity is common in western popular culture, '[m]ale virginity not only must be lost; it must be lost as quickly as possible'. If not, the man becomes a failure or an object of ridicule. Allan's survey finds two common explanations for prolonged virginity: either the man is mentally or physically ill, or he is a genius and out of touch with his sexuality. In a supernatural world, there is a third choice: the man has become a woman.

None of these conditions describes Dean, until his resurrection. He returns with no marks of his violent death or the torture he experienced in hell. The scars of old injuries have also disappeared, so Dean assumes experiences don't carry over from one life to the next. Consequently, he proclaims he has been 'rehymenated' and attempts to mitigate the double monstrosity of having a hymen (a body part belonging to a woman) and having years of sexual conquests erased (along with proof of his virility). Dean's fear of virginity is emblematic of the fear of castration: if he is a virgin, then he must also be a woman; if he is a woman, he no longer possesses a phallus. He tells Sam 'the dude will not abide' and pursues an attractive waitress in the hopes of devirginizing himself

Figure 5: A montage of
shirtless RoboSam's morning
workout from 'The Third Man'.

('Monster Movie' [Season 4, Episode 5]).

Like Dean, Sam returns from the dead symbolically castrated. Instead of virginity, Sam's castration occurs through the absence of his soul. RoboSam, as this soulless version is known among fans, engages in behaviours the 'real' Sam never would: he has sex with a prostitute, watches while Dean gets hurt, and ruthlessly murders those he is supposed to protect. Without a soul to fill his body, Sam becomes monstrous. As despicable as the canon makes RoboSam, fans frequently praise his sex appeal. In one notable scene, RoboSam works out without a shirt, with close-ups on his muscular chest and back ('The Third Man' [Season 6, Episode 3]). Suzette Chan observes that in Season 4, Sam's addiction to demon blood leads to increased psychic powers, which are 'visually represented by Sam's imposing demon-smiting physique'.[6] While the series depicts Sam's demon blood addiction and his soullessness as monstrous, both storylines enable fans to celebrate the male hard body. After the shirtless workout scene, fans created icons and animated gifs with taglines like 'I love you, Sera Gamble' (the season's show-runner) and the more sarcastic 'I watch it for the plot.' Thus, when Sam is at his most monstrous, his body is most obviously on display for the female gaze – reaffirming the desirability of the monstrous male body narrative.

### 'They're all inside me, millions upon millions of souls'[7]

Unlike Dean and Sam's castration through absence, Castiel's body shows the horror of excess. He swallows countless souls from purgatory, and in a visual reference to the film *Alien*, the souls are seen pushing against Castiel's stomach from the inside, desperate to get out ('Meet the New Boss' [Season 7, Episode 1]). The double-occupancy – the souls inside the angel Castiel inside the body of Jimmy Novak – is a monstrous turn that damages Castiel's relationship with the Winchesters and ultimately causes his demise. Jimmy Novak's body deteriorates because it is not strong enough to house the souls,

## The Monstrous Male Body
Bridget Kies

*Figure 6: Following 'Meet the New Boss,' fans declared, 'Canon mpreg!'*

or, in horror terms, because the male body is incapable of sustaining pregnancy. Castiel is killed by the monsters inside him as they struggle to break free. While the series codes this as the meaningless death of a hero who reaches too high, we can also read it as a fitting conclusion to a horror narrative of a male body turned into a monstrous-feminine womb.

Male pregnancy stories are more widely explored in the fandom. Known as 'mpreg', these stories are not exclusive to Castiel, and most don't end tragically. The pregnancy sometimes occurs as a result of supernatural forces, such as a witch's curse, and sometimes it is just part of the unexplained background world of the story. In her investigation of mpreg in the *Supernatural* fandom, Berit Åström finds that emotional outbursts considered effeminate and undesirable in the series are common, as is a feeling of satisfaction at becoming a father/mother. While this is not true for all stories, Åström notes that these instances clash with 'the popular culture image of what a young man should be, and [with] the canon's image of masculinity'. Female fans who read and write mpreg derive pleasure in refiguring the male body into the feminine, thus challenging common assumptions about masculinity both in canon and in society. In some stories, the characters even settle down to raise their families, thus turning the monstrosity into a happily ever after.

## Conclusion
While this is not an exhaustive list, these examples demonstrate how the male body is rendered into the monstrous-feminine in *Supernatural*, to the horror of the characters and to the delight of fans. To understand the source of this delight, we might consider Freud's claim that the distinction between pleasure and pain can become blurred, if not irrelevant. Leo Bersani puts it this way: 'What would it mean to say that in sexuality, pleasure is somehow distinct from satisfaction, perhaps even identical to a kind of pain?' (p. 34). In the case of *Supernatural*, we see how the monstrous-feminine is painful for the male Winchesters and pleasurable for their largely female fan base. But as fictional characters, Sam and Dean will survive whatever traumas are thrown at them. Fans are the ones who genuinely suffer as they empathize with their beloved characters, but that suffering is part of the pleasure of being a fan of the show. ●

## GO FURTHER

### Books

*Phallic Panic*,
Barbara Creed
(Melbourne: MUP, 2005)

*The Monstrous-Feminine*
Barbara Creed
(New York: Routledge, 1993)

*The Freudian Body*
Leo Bersani
(New York: Columbia University Press, 1986)

### Extracts/Essays/Articles

'Theorising Male Virginity in Popular Romance Novels'
Jonathan Allan
In *Journal of Popular Romance Studies*. 2: 1 (2011) [Online], http://jprstudies.
org/2011/10/theorising-male-virginity/.

'Let's Get Those Winchesters Pregnant: Male Pregnancy in *Supernatural* Fan Fiction'
Berit Åström
In *Transformative Works and Cultures*. 4 (2010) [Online], http://dx.doi.org/10.3983/
twc.2010.0135.

'*Supernatural* Bodies: Writing Subjugation and Resistance onto Sam and Dean
Winchester'
Suzanne Chan
In *Transformative Works and Cultures*. 4 (2010) [Online], http://dx.doi.org/10.3983/
twc.2010.0179.

'A Boy for All Planets: *Roswell*, *Smallville*, and the Teen Male Melodrama'
Miranda J. Banks
In Glyn Davis and Kay Dickinson (eds). *Teen TV: Genre, Consumption, and Identity*
(London: BFI, 2004), pp. 17–28.

'Visual Pleasure and Narrative Cinema'

**The Monstrous Male Body**
Bridget Kies

Laura Mulvey
In *Screen*. 16: 3 (1975), pp. 6-18.

'The Passing of the Oedipus Complex'
Sigmund Freud in *International Journal of Psycho-Analysis*. 5:4 (1924), pp. 419-24.

**Film/Television**

*Supernatural*, Eric Kripke, creator (Los Angeles: Warner Brothers, 2005-).

'In My Time of Dying', Kim Manners, dir. *Supernatural*
(Los Angeles: Warner Brothers, 2006)

'The Rapture', Charles Beeson, dir. *Supernatural* (Los Angeles: Warner Brothers, 2006)
'I Believe the Children Are Our Future', Charles Beeson, dir. *Supernatural* (Los Angeles: Warner Brothers, 2006)

'Devil's Trap', Kim Manners, dir. *Supernatural* (Los Angeles: Warner Brothers, 2006)

'Are You There God? It's Me, Dean Winchester', Philip Sgriccia, dir. *Supernatural*
(Los Angeles: Warner Brothers, 2006)

'Born Under a Bad Sign', J. Miller Tobin, dir. *Supernatural*
(Los Angeles: Warner Brothers, 2006)

'The Monster at the End of This Book', Mike Rohl, dir. *Supernatural*
(Los Angeles: Warner Brothers, 2006)

'Jus in Bello',  Philip Sgriccia, dir. *Supernatural* (Los Angeles: Warner Brothers, 2006)

'Swan Song', Steve Boyum, dir. *Supernatural* (Los Angeles: Warner Brothers, 2006)

'Lazarus Rising',  Kim Manners, dir. *Supernatural* (Los Angeles: Warner Brothers, 2006)

'The Magnificent Seven', Kim Manners, dir. *Supernatural*
(Los Angeles: Warner Brothers, 2006)

'Monster Movie', Robert Singer, dir. *Supernatural* (Los Angeles: Warner Brothers, 2006)

'The Third Man', Robert Singer, dir. *Supernatural* (Los Angeles: Warner Brothers, 2006)

'Meet the New Boss', Philip Sgriccia, dir. *Supernatural*
(Los Angeles: Warner Brothers, 2006)

**Online**

'Why We LOVE Jensen Ackles!'
athomemomblog (pseud.)
*Squidoo*. ND, http://www.squidoo.com/jensen-ackles#module3566687.

'Interview: Sera Gamble, Producer and Writer for *Supernatural*'
C. P. Cochran
*Firefox News*. March 1, 2008, http://firefox.org/news/articles/1254/1/Interview-Sera-Gamble-Producer-and-Writer-for-quotSupernaturalquot/Page1.html.

'Fan Tattoos'. *Supernatural* Wiki, Last updated January 2, 2013, http://www.supernaturalwiki.com/index.php?title=Fan_Tattoos.

**Notes**

(Endnotes)
1 In fact, the phenomenon is not limited to *Supernatural*: 'CW pretty boy' is a common expression for the network's casting of young, attractive men with slightly feminized features. Using *Smallville* (Jerry Siegel, WB, 2001-2011) as an example, Miranda J. Banks describes how these 'pretty boys' represent a new kind of male hero.

2 For a fuller understanding of the gaze, see Laura Mulvey's essay, 'Cinematic Representation and Visual Pleasure' (1975). Mulvey asserts that film is an extension of the male gaze that objectifies the female body. Series like *Supernatural*, with male leads and a predominantly female fan base, subvert this phenomenon.

3 Dean to Sam in 'Born Under a Bad Sign' (Season 2, Episode 14).

4 Although the story of the possession leading to pregnancy is only told through a brief flashback, it raises interesting questions about the series' mythology. How does a non-corporeal demon inseminate a human? Does this constitute asexual reproduction? The hybrid child, Jesse, disappears at the conclusion of the episode, neatly allowing Sam and Dean to avoid killing a child, though fans wisely decry this lack of narrative closure and take up the mantle in metas and fanfiction. Jesse's very existence is an example of a monstrous male, and his mother's pregnancy is a classic horror film representation of the monstrous womb.

5 Dean to Sam in 'Monster Movie' (Season 4, Episode 5).

6 Jared Padalecki has explained in several interviews that, in reality, his increased stature was the result of him bulking up for his role in *Friday the 13th* (Marcus Nispel dir. 2009)

7 Castiel, speaking of the souls from purgatory that he has swallowed, 'The Man Who Knew Too Much' (Season 6, Episode 22).

# 'THERE'S SAM GIRLS AND DEAN GIRLS AND...WHAT'S A SLASH FAN?'

**DEAN TO SAM IN
'THE MONSTER AT THE END OF THIS BOOK'
SEASON 4, EPISODE 18**

Chapter
3

# I See What You Did There: *SPN* and the Fourth Wall

## Lisa Macklem

→ The way viewers interact with television has changed remarkably in the last decade. Julie D'Acci points out 'the impact of new technologies, especially the Internet', on television and suggests the need to incorporate new ways of thinking about television that are 'dedicated to analyzing the inter-workings of industries, programming, and everyday life' (p. 421). Lynn Zubernis and Katherine Larsen have just concluded a more than five-year study of the *Supernatural* fandom and identify that:

> The relationship between fans and the creative side, as well as the human representations of the fannish objects themselves, are increasingly reciprocal. [...] With face-to-face interaction at conventions, the hierarchical boundaries separating fans and fannish objects begin to break down. Even more strikingly, the advent of Twitter, Facebook, and instant feedback ensures that the relationship between fans and creators is no longer unidirectional. (p. 14)

Given its devoted and enthusiastic fan base, it is not surprising that *Supernatural* has bridged the relatively small space separating its audience and characters. Sera Gamble, showrunner for Seasons 6 and 7, states that 'something unique about the show *Supernatural* is the quality of the fanbase. We have always been in a pretty direct dialogue with our fans through the show'. Gamble and writer/producer Ben Edlund discussed how they were able to breach the wall that traditionally stands between an audience and the cultural artefact. Gamble says:

> You have a fanbase that is loyal [...] and you're thankful that they're loyal and the least that we can do is do an episode that acknowledges that they know more than the average viewer about the show [...] You're rewarded for your diligence as a fan.

Edlund (2010) remarks that he

> didn't feel like [...] I was making a gift for the fans. It was more like we were taking part in this weird relationship that we have with the fans. It was like we could depend on the fans to sort of understand because this is a very specific situation: this *Supernatural*, the show, the audience, and how this functions.

In fact, Edlund goes on to distinguish *Supernatural* fans from fans of other shows: '*Supernatural* fandom is a really phenomenologically [sic] amazing thing. I've been in other situations, viewed other versions of fandom and [...] [this is] amazing.'

 *Supernatural* has broken the fourth wall often to comment on itself and the entertainment industry. It has also incorporated insider jokes that depend on the deep and specific knowledge of its fan base. Finally, the show has also drawn its audience and fans through the fourth wall to be a part of the story itself.

 Any time the audience is reminded that they are watching a show, or are drawn more directly into the action, can be seen as breaking that fictional barrier between audience and artefact, between audience and character. Gamble and Edlund discuss this on the commentary track at the end of 'The French Mistake'(Season 6, Episode 15), in which actors Padalecki and Ackles play characters Sam and Dean portraying actors Padalecki and Ackles. Edlund expresses concern over 'lifting the veil' and revealing the magic. Gamble hopes that having pulled back the curtain on the nuts and bolts of television

**I See What You Did There: *SPN* and the Fourth Wall**
Lisa Macklem

*Figure 1: Sam and Dean play
Jared and Jensen in 'The
French Mistake'*

production and the show itself has not 'ruined'
the viewing experience for the audience.

This can be referred to as a technique of
metafiction, the self-conscious reference of fictional devices within fiction or, in this
case, television as television. It takes a special relationship to be able to do this without
alienating the audience, and *Supernatural* relies on viewers having behind-the-scenes
knowledge of the show and its production. *Supernatural*, in fact, has managed to draw
its audience closer. Henry Jenkins has used the term 'participatory culture' which he
'contrasts with older notions of passive media spectatorship' (p. 3). June Deery also
comments on this new relationship:

Viewers may now join a community of critical readers whose attention to the show's
production and to the program as artifact may in fact alter the ontological status of
the show-as-perceived-by-viewers, producing a postmodern self-reflexivity – what Um-
berto Eco has termed 'neo-television' – even when this self-consciousness was not embedded in the show by its producers. (p. 175)

This new relationship allows for viewers to deepen their experience; it allows them to
enter the show itself in new ways.

## Self-parody

Some of *Supernatural*'s most successful episodes that break the fourth wall are those
in which the writers parody or critique themselves. There are few episodes of *Supernatural*, in fact, that do not contain at least a wink to the attentive fan. Arguably, the first
episode to at least address the fourth wall was Season 2's 'Hollywood Babylon' (Season 2,
Episode 18) in which the two brothers investigate a haunting on a movie set. The writers
use the premise to explore some of the issues that the show had faced in relation to production pressures. While this episode does not employ any characters talking directly to
the camera, it does rely on viewers having 'inside' knowledge of the show. In one scene,
the studio executive says to the director: 'Everyone at the studio loves the dailies, myself included. We were just wondering if it could be a little brighter.' The director replies,
'Brad, this is a horror movie.' To which the studio executive responds, 'Who says horror
has to be dark? It's sort of depressing, don't you think?' This is based on actual notes
that the *Supernatural* production received from Warner Brothers executives. Naturally
the show is quite deliberately dark and atmospheric, reflecting and enhancing the subject matter – a feature very much appreciated by its fans.

There are a number of other shout-outs to members of the *Supernatural* Family in
'Hollywood Babylon'. Dean has a fan-moment with Tara, the star of the movie, and tells
her that he loved her in *Boogeyman* (dir. Stephen T. Kay, 2005). She responds, 'What a
terrible script, but thank you!' The joke is that the creator of *Supernatural*, Eric Kripke,

Figure 2: 'Hollywood Babylon'

Figure 3: The Death of Kripke,
'The French Mistake'

wrote *Boogeyman*. There are other significant self-reflex-ive references. The director mentions 'Ivan and the other FX guys', a reference to Ivan Hayden, the visual effects su-pervisor. The director in the episode is McG, an executive producer on the show. The fake trailer for *Hell Hazers II* in the middle of the episode references the two *Charlie's Angels* movies (2000, 2003) that the real McG directed.

The industry itself, particularly genre television, is paro-died again in 'Changing Channels' (Season 5, Episode 8), where Dean and Sam are trapped in an alternate 'televi-sion' universe by the Trickster. While trapped in a sitcom, Dean turns to the camera with his catch phrase 'sonu-vabitch' but says it in a way to garner laughs, letting the audience in on the joke. The entire 'Changing Channels' episode allowed the show to provide commentary on the television industry, critiquing such television fare as *CSI Miami* (Anthony E. Zuiker, CBS, 2002-2011), Japanese game shows, commercials and *Grey's Anatomy* (Shonda Rhimes, ABC, 2005 - ), Sam also addresses the camera directly in the Herpaxia commercial. The overall structure of this episode follows the brothers' own trajectory, jumping from drama to comedy to game show. The Trickster, who one expects to subject the brothers to comic discomfort, keeps admonishing the brothers to play their roles.

'The French Mistake' takes the self-parodic moments to new heights by focusing on the dysfunctional set of the television series '*Supernatural*'. Several cast and crew members: Lou Bollo, the stunt coordinator; Misha Collins; Genevieve Padalecki; and stuntmen Todd Scott and Mike Carpenter; play themselves – albeit parodies of them-selves. Throughout the commentary on the Blu-ray, the audience is repeatedly told that this is not how the actual people are in real life. Actors play the rest of the crew, but virtually every crew member volunteered to have their stand-in shot (and killed) in the massacre scene. On the commentary track, Gamble credits Tina Fey and *30 Rock* (Tina Fey, NBC, 2006-2013) for guidance in how to parody herself and the other members of the production team. Gamble also notes that 'the reason we can do this episode [...] [is] because we were confident that [the audience] were interested on some level in how the show is made'. The episode does provide unprecedented access to the inner work-ings of the show.

Some of the details for 'characters' were drawn from real life, such as director Bob Singer's fondness for Diet Coke and Eric Kripke's insistence that his stand-in wear New Balance running shoes, not Nikes. The casting directors for the show were initially con-cerned about the reception by the real people of the actors cast to play them, according to Gamble. Everyone was pleased with the final result, however, and no one more than

**I See What You Did There: *SPN* and the Fourth Wall**
Lisa Macklem

*Figure 4: Leviathan Sam and Dean in 'Slash Fiction'*

*Figure 5: Castiel, 'The Man Who Would Be King'*

Kripke, who was particularly fond of his death scene – a hero's death.

The episode also alludes to other industry-specific jokes. There are many infamous stories about co-stars not getting along, explaining references to 'at least they're talking'. It is well known, however, that Ackles and Padalecki are good friends. At one point, Bob Singer asks them if giving them more money will get them back to work. Dean remarks that they are already paid too much – the irony is obvious. The studio in which the fictional show is shot is KM Studios – a shout-out to Kim Manners who executive produced and oversaw production for the first four seasons of the show, right up until his death. The unflappable French Canadian director of photography, Serge Ladouceur, is seen with his ever present laser pen. When the massacre happens, he is seen calmly dodging bullets and is one of the few crew members to escape death.

Misha Collins has a particularly unique and close relationship with the fans, and has a strong Twitter following. For 'The French Mistake', Collins asked the writers to make him as 'douchy' as possible. He is seen tweeting his fans obsessively. In keeping with the meta-textual nature of the episode, Collins live-tweeted the same tweets that his character was tweeting during the episode on both east and west coast feeds of the original airing.

## Insider jokes

Both Sam and Dean address the audience in 'The French Mistake'. In another episode, 'Slash Fiction' (Season 7, Episode 6), Leviathan (monster) versions of Sam and Dean also speak directly into the camera. The episode begins with what appears to the viewer to be the real Sam and Dean robbing a bank. Just before the brothers kill all the hostages, Dean looks at the security camera, smiles and winks. Dean is looking directly at the camera and the viewer, a signal to the audience that this is not really Dean; in essence, the wink letting the viewer into the 'joke'.

In 'The Man Who Would Be King' (Season 6, Episode 20), Castiel addresses the audience directly to explain the actions that have occurred off-camera in Season 6. He says 'Let me tell you my story', and then looks directly at the camera before delivering his next line: 'Let me tell you everything.' Season 6 was not the show's most popular season, and Castiel's plea for understanding may be a plea from the writers for understanding from the audience.

Insider jokes or 'Easter eggs' are another way that *Supernatural* invites the fans in

*Figure 6: Supernatural Easter Eggs*

---

*Figure 7: Alan and Jensen Ackles in 'Heartache'*

and rewards them for their attention to detail. In 'Hollywood Babylon', Sam complains that the weather is 'practically Canadian', a wink to the fact that the show is shot in Canada. Later, there's a fake trailer for a Season 1 episode of *Supernatural* featuring a killer 'monster truck'.

Casual viewers are unlikely to realize that the picture of the Grand Marshall on the banner in 'Good God Y'All' (Season 5, Episode 2), really is Jerry Wanek, the production designer for the show, or that Sam and Dean drink Margiekugel beer, named for Wanek's mother.

Bobby Singer is named after executive producer Robert Singer. The character Jamie in the episode 'Monster Movie' (Season 4, Episode 5) is named after a fan who wrote to Kripke telling him how much the show meant to her and helped her deal with an ongoing illness. Another fan, author S. E. Hinton, is an extra in 'Slash Fiction'. Her novel *The Outsiders* (1967) has also been referenced obliquely in the show in 'Death Takes a Holiday'. Dean's favourite show 'Dr. Sexy MD', the *Grey's Anatomy* spoof, references a ghost on the show. The inside joke is that the ghost on *Grey's* was played by Jeffrey Dean Morgan, who also played John Winchester.

In 'The Man Who Would Be King', there is a demon equivalent to Bobby (Jim Beaver) who is called Ellesworth, Beaver's character on *Deadwood* (David Milch, HBO, 2004-2006). Fans would recognize Louden Swain's music in the episode 'Slice Girls'(Season 7, Episode 13) – lead singer Rob Benedict played Chuck Shirley in Seasons 4 and 5. Fans are also invited into the episodes that Jensen Ackles has directed. The episode 'Weekend at Bobby's' (Season 6, Episode 4), Ackles's directorial debut, opens with a television newscast playing in the background. The voice-over in the newscast was done by Ackles's father, Alan. In Season 8's 'Heartache' (Season 8, Episode 3), Alan Ackles is a guest star, and Donna Ackles, Jensen's mother, is in the background.

In 'The Girl Next Door' (Season 7, Episode 3), there are two shout-outs to other Ackles projects. A clerk is wearing a *Batman, Under the Red Hood* (dir. Brandon Vietti, 2010) T-shirt, an animated film for which Ackles supplied one of the voices. When Sam slips away and leaves Dean in the cabin, the television is announcing the movie about to play as 'My Bloodiest Valentine in 3D'. Ackles starred in the 3D thriller *My Bloody Valentine* (dir. Patrick Lussier, 2009). A viewer does not have to know about these connections to understand or enjoy the story, but it adds another level of reward for viewers who have that depth of knowledge.

*Supernatural* breaks the fourth wall, perhaps most significantly, in 'The Monster at the End of This Book' (Season 4, Episode 18). With this episode, the show brings the fans and the audience right into the world of *Supernatural* when Dean and Sam discover a

**I See What You Did There: *SPN* and the Fourth Wall**
Lisa Macklem

*Figure 8: 'The Monster at the End of This Book'*

*Figure 9: 'Swan Song'*

series of books have been published about their lives. The author of the books is Carver Edlund, a combination of show writers Jeremy Carver and Ben Edlund, and the publisher is Sera Siege, a combination of writers Sera Gamble and Julie Siege. The publisher's protectiveness of Carver Edlund's real identity in the face of 'bad' fans, can also been seen as a parallel for the passion the *Supernatural* fandom has for its artefact. It turns out that the novels are no longer being printed because there were not enough fans to keep them in print. This parallels the nervous wait for *Supernatural* to be renewed each season.

Sam and Dean's discovery of the fandom and the books gives the actors and the show a unique way to have a discussion with, and about, the fans. The brothers discover the online commu-nity of fans, fanfiction and specifically the phe-nomenon of Wincest (fanworks romantically pairing the Winchester brothers). Both are appalled by this, prompting Dean to ask 'They do know we're brothers, right?' They also discover fan Simpatico, an actual poster on *Television Without Pity.com*, who was even-tually banned for posting overly negative posts.

By the end of the episode, Dean and Sam discover that Chuck Shirley – Carver Ed-lund's 'real' name – is a prophet. Chuck is a little reluctant to believe it, but finally says, 'I write things and then they come to life. Yeah, no, I'm definitely a god. A cruel, cruel, capricious god.' This foreshadows the eventual revelation that Chuck *is* God, and a metaphor for Kripke, the one who initially created the show and brought Dean and Sam to life. It is no accident that Chuck disappears into the light at the end of 'Swan Song' (Season 5, Episode 22) – the last episode that Kripke was showrunner. The voice-over in 'Swan Song' is an opportunity for Kripke to break the fourth wall and address fans almost directly.

The fans are addressed again in the Season 5 opener, 'Sympathy for the Devil' (Sea-son 5, Episode 1), with the introduction of Becky, the super-fan. Chuck asks her to de-liver a message to Sam and Dean. In effect, by telling her that Sam and Dean Winchester are real, he has broken the fourth wall into the novels. Fan response to Becky was mixed. Her portrayal is a little over the top, she has few and poor social skills and is not fash-ionably dressed. When she meets Sam, she is almost hyperventilating and will not stop touching him. Her discomfiture is typical of fans meeting the object of their fannish passions and is similar to the way Dean acts when he meets Dr. Sexy. Becky was most objected to by 'Samgirls', likely because she herself is an aggressive Sam-fan. In the end, however, she provides valuable information for the brothers and serves a useful function in the episode.

Some fans felt they were being mocked, but it is significant that the show had already essentially mocked both itself and the studios which are its direct superiors. In 'The Real Ghostbusters' (Season 5, Episode 9), Dean and Sam are tricked by Becky into attending the first ever fan convention for the Carver Edlund novels. Throughout the course of the episode, however, the brothers learn something about the fans and the fans help them gain a new perspective on their own story. Again, this mirrors the close relationship between the show and its fans. Dean, in particular, has been struggling to find the purpose in what they do, and Barnes and Demian, who are LARPing (live action role playing) as Sam and Dean, offer that purpose:

You're wrong, you know. About *Supernatural*. I'm not sure you get what the story's about. In real life? He sells stereo equipment. I fix copiers. *Our* lives suck. But to be Sam and Dean? To wake up every morning and save the world? To have a brother who would die for you. Well, who wouldn't want that?

Barnes explains to Dean what makes the books popular to fans, speaking as the writers, letting fans of the show know that the writers understand what the core of appeal is for them. Dean is a little taken aback when he finds out that Barnes and Demian are a couple, but he also has grudging respect for why they have come together to form such a strong partnership and it helps him shore up his flagging motivation to keep going in the hunt for Lucifer.

Here again the show is referencing Wincest and slash fanfiction, but in a more sympathetic way. Becky has finally turned her sights on a more appropriate love interest in Chuck in this episode, and she proves to be extremely useful when her encyclopedic knowledge of the books allows her to help the brothers locate the weapon they hope will kill Lucifer. A much less flattering version of Becky emerges in 'Season Seven, Time for a Wedding!' (Season 7, Episode 8) when she stoops to using a love potion to trick Sam into marrying her. Becky is portrayed as a loser, despite her knowledge of hunting through reading the novels, which is also showcased in the episode. Becky tries to explain her actions to Sam:

I know what I am, okay. I'm a loser. In school. In life [...] Honestly? The only place people understood me was the message boards. They were grumpy and overly literal but at least we shared a common passion. And I'll take it, you know? I met you guys. The real Sam and Dean. And I started dating Chuck. And everything was amazing. But you left and Chuck dumped me.

This speech does paint a more sympathetic view of what fandom can offer: a place

## I See What You Did There: *SPN* and the Fourth Wall
Lisa Macklem

*Figure 10: Becky with a tied up Sam, 'Season Seven, Time for a Wedding!'*

*Figure 11: "Dean reacts to Dr. Sexy, M.D. in 'Changing Channels'"*

where fans feel they can belong. However, it also intimates that that sense of belonging is fleeting and will prove to be unsatisfying. In the end, Sam tells her that he likely will not see her again, but he does take pity on her somewhat and tells her, 'You're not a loser, ok? You're a good person and you've got lots of energy so just do your thing, whatever that is, and the right guy will find you.' This episode seems to focus on the fan who is too immersed in the show. This curiously bitter version of fandom comes at a time when Gamble was under siege from fans who were not happy about the direction she was taking with the show. Fan reaction to this version of Becky saw this as a negative comment from the show about fans which did not seem consistent with the previous incarnations of Becky and fandom in general, and many fans refuse to acknowledge this episode as part of canon.

In contrast, Dean is established as a fanboy in his own right in 'Hollywood Babylon' and in 'Changing Channels'. 'Dr. Sexy MD' is Dean's guilty pleasure, but the fact that he knows Dr. Sexy should be wearing cowboy boots – 'they're what make him sexy' – is an important detail in helping the brothers solve their situation in the episode; being a fan is cast in a positive light. In 'Frontierland' (Season 6, Episode 18), the object of Dean's fannish passion is Clint Eastwood, and in 'Time After Time' (Season 7, Episode 12), Dean is able to work with another of his heroes: Elliot Ness. Dean's fannish behaviour is usually a bit over the top and given comic overtones, but in an endearing way. In most encounters, Dean is faced with a disparity between the reality and the illusion, much as any fan must deal with a disparity between character and actor.

## Conclusion

*Supernatural* has the singular ability to engage its audience in a dialogue. Jenkins states that

convergence represents a paradigm shift – a move from medium-specific content toward content that flows across multiple media channels, toward the increased interdependence of communications systems, toward multiple ways of accessing media content, and toward ever more complex relations between top-down corporate media and bottom-up participatory culture. (p. 243)

*Supernatural* relies on its fans to understand what is at play between the show and its viewers. ●

~~~~~~~~~

## GO FURTHER

### Books

*Fandom at the Crossroads: Celebration, Shame and Fan/Producer Relationships*
Lynn Zubernis and Katherine Larsen
(Newcastle upon Tyne: Cambridge Scholars Publishing, 2012)

*Convergence Culture*
Henry Jenkins
(New York: NYUP, 2006)

### Extracts/Essays/Articles

'Watching Television Without Pity: The Productivity of Online Fans'
Mark Anrejevic
In *Television & New Media*. 9: 1 (2008), pp. 24–46.

'Cultural Outlaws: An Examination of Audience Activity and Online Television Fandom'
Victor Costello and Barbara Moore
In *Television & New Media*. 8: 2 (2007), pp.124–43.

'Cultural Studies, Television Studies, and the Crisis in the Humanities' Julie D'Acci
In Lynn Spigel and Jan Olsson (eds). *Television After TV: Essays on a Medium in Transition* (Durham: Duke University Press, 2004, pp. 418-486).

'TV.com: Participatory Viewing on the Web'
June Deery
In *The Journal of Popular Culture*. 37: 2 (2003), pp.161-83.

### Film/Television

'The French Mistake', Charles Beeson, dir. *Supernatural*
(Los Angeles: Warner Brothers, 2011)

'Hollywood Babylon', Philip Sgriccia, dir. *Supernatural*
(Los Angeles: Warner Brothers, 2007)

'Changing Channels', Charles Beeson, dir. *Supernatural*
(Los Angeles: Warner Brothers, 2009)

**I See What You Did There:** *SPN* **and the Fourth Wall**
Lisa Macklem

'Slash Fiction', John Showalter, dir. *Supernatural* (Los Angeles: Warner Brothers, 2011)

'The Man Who Would Be King', Ben Edlund, dir. *Supernatural*
(Los Angeles: Warner Brothers, 2011)

'Good God, Y'All', Philip Sgriccia, dir. *Supernatural* (Los Angeles: Warner Brothers, 2009)

'Devil's Trap', Kim Manners, dir. *Supernatural* (Los Angeles: Warner Brothers, 2006)

'Monster Movie', Robert Singer, dir. *Supernatural* (Los Angeles: Warner Brothers,

'Slice Girls', Jerry Wanek, dir. *Supernatural* (Los Angeles: Warner Brothers, 2012)

'Weekend at Bobby's', Jensen Ackles, dir. *Supernatural*
(Los Angeles: Warner Brothers, 2010)

'Heartache', Jensen Ackles, dir. *Supernatural* (Los Angeles: Warner Brothers, 2012)

'The Girl Next Door', Jensen Ackles, dir. *Supernatural*
(Los Angeles: Warner Brothers, 2011)

'The Monster at the End of This Book', Mike Rohl, dir. *Supernatural*
(Los Angeles: Warner Brothers, 2009).

'Swan Song', Steve Boyum, dir. *Supernatural* (Los Angeles: Warner Brothers, 2010)

'Sympathy for the Devil', Robert Singer, dir. *Supernatural*
(Los Angeles: Warner Brothers, 2009)

'The Real Ghostbusters', James L. Conway, dir. *Supernatural*
(Los Angeles: Warner Brothers, 2009)

'Season Seven, Time for a Wedding!', Tim Andrew, dir. *Supernatural*
(Los Angeles: Warner Brothers, 2011)

'Time After Time', Philip Sgriccia, dir. *Supernatural* (Los Angeles: Warner Brothers, 2012)

'Frontierland', Guy Norman Bee, dir. *Supernatural* (Los Angeles: Warner Brothers, 2011)

*Supernatural*, Eric Kripke, creator (Los Angeles: Warner Brothers, 2005–)

'THE ONLY PLACE
PEOPLE UNDERSTOOD
ME WAS ON THE
MESSAGE BOARDS.
THEY WERE GRUMPY
AND OVERLY LITERAL,
BUT AT LEAST WE
SHARED A COMMON
PASSION.'

**SEASON SEVEN,
'TIME FOR A WEDDING'**
SEASON 7, EPISODE 8

Chapter
4

# Post, Reblog, Follow, Tweet: *Supernatural* Fandom and Social Media

Jules Wilkinson

→ **Yeah, MySpace, what the hell is that? Seriously, is that like some sort of porn site? (Dean, 'Crossroad Blues' Season 2, Episode 8)**

When the first episode of *Supernatural* aired on 13 September 2005, the Internet looked very different. MySpace was the most popular social networking site, YouTube had only been around for six months and Mark Zuckerberg was still wondering if his Facebook might be popular with people other than horny college kids. The iPhone was still two years away. Back then, the term web 2.0 had just started to gain currency to describe a new form of Internet infrastructure. Just like fandom, web 2.0 – or social media as it became known – is all about connecting people and collaborative creation, not just the individual, passive consumption of content. Fandom and social media is a match made in cyberspace.

I have been part of the *Supernatural* fandom as we've grown from a small following of a genre show on the smallest network into a global phenomenon, with a huge creative output, dozens of conventions held on four continents and a show that looks certain to run ten seasons. It might be impossible to untangle how social media shaped our fandom, or indeed how our activities shaped the use of social media. Like any good partnership, fans and social media together produced synergies that bring out the best in both of them. Our fandom is a large, extended, slightly dysfunctional family. Like Sam and Dean, we all have our own version of family history and this is the online history of mine.

**The only place people understood me was on the message boards. They were grumpy and overly literal but at least we shared a common passion. (Becky, 'Season Seven, Time for a Wedding!' Season 7, Episode 8)**
By the time I watched the Pilot of *Supernatural* on Australian television in February 2006, the *Supernatural* fandom was already settling down with social media and picking out curtains. The show itself had been part of developing that relationship. Warner Brothers had paired with Yahoo and made the Pilot of *Supernatural* free via streaming for a week ahead of the official airing on The WB on 14 September 2005. According to David Janollari at *Futon Critic.com*, Entertainment Head at Warner Brothers, this was designed 'to break through the clutter of other media and help reach the savvy young viewing audience that we know will embrace *Supernatural*'. Oh, to be young and savvy again!

During the first three seasons of *Supernatural*, the major centres of the fandom were on LiveJournal (LJ), message boards on fandom-specific websites such as *Supernatural.tv* and *Winchester Bros.com*, and on the forums of media sites including the WB and later the CW websites, *Tv.com* and *Television Without Pity.com*. MySpace and Facebook had only a small fandom presence, as fans tended to keep a separation between their personal blogs on those sites, and their online fannish presence. In those early years, fans tended to stick to one site and it was possible to feel that wherever you were was the centre of *Supernatural* fandom. Each forum or community had its own cultural mores, in-jokes and etiquette. These were not always easy to discern – I think I was banned three times from the *Television Without Pity* forums without having any idea what rules I'd transgressed.

Some phenomena were common across fan communities. Wherever there were fans, there were Sam girls and Dean girls – fans strongly aligned to one or the other of the brothers – who would protest any perceived slights against the character by other

**Post, Reblog, Follow, Tweet: *Supernatural* Fandom and Social Media**
Jules Wilkinson

fans, characters or the writers. Fannish vernacular and memes crossed between sites. The nickname Metallicar for the iconic Impala originated on 11 October 2005 on the *Supernatural* thread on *Television Without Pity* and was soon in common use throughout fandom. It later began appearing on merchandise, and was even used by creator Eric Kripke in the commentary on the Season Two DVD.

My experience of *Supernatural* fandom has been largely shaped by two quite different social media sites. LJ has given me an intense, full body immersion experience of the fandom, and as administrator of the *Supernatural* Wiki, I've gained a broader view of just how diverse the fandom is.

### No, I really can't read your LJ short story. I get it – Sam and Dean really love each other. I just don't need to see that. (Chuck, deleted scene, 'The Real Ghostbusters' Season 5, Episode 9)

LJ was one of the first social blogging sites, and from its inception in 1999 has been a popular base for many fandoms. It offers personal blogs and multi-user ones known as communities, and makes it easy to post text, photos and video. These features resulted in it becoming the largest single site for creative works in the *Supernatural* fandom, a position it still holds, although it is now a smaller fish in a much larger pond. On LJ, *Supernatural* attracted fans from other fandoms such as *Smallville* (Jerry Siegel WB, 2001-2011), *Stargate* (Jonathan Glassner and Brad Wright, Showtime, 1997-2007) and DC Comics. These fans knew that it takes a (cyber) village to raise a fandom. They set up communities, ran challenges and hosted friending memes. They brought with them the knowledge of how to make a group of fans into a community and build an infrastructure that leveraged the basic format of LJ to meet our needs.

By the time I joined the fandom in January 2006, LJ fandom was a vibrant and thriving community. By October that year, the LJ *Supernatural* fandom held its first meet-up at WinchesterCon, a fan-only convention held in Nashville that attracted nearly 200 fans. Since that time, LJ has hosted just about every type of creative fan endeavour one could imagine. The sheer volume and diversity of creativity is staggering. In events such as the *SPN/J2 Big Bang* challenge which started in 2007, fans have produced over 1,000 novel-length stories and accompanying artworks. At the end of Season 2 another fan, anteka, and I self-published the first collection of essays about the show, *Some of Us Really Do Watch for the Plot* (2007), with contributions from around forty fans from LJ. I even once hosted a *Supernatural*-themed baking challenge.

The first serious challenge to LJ as a major fannish site came in May 2007 in what became known as 'LJ Strikethrough'. A group purportedly trying to protect children from online predators, asked LJ to remove sites which they saw as offensive. The owners of LJ responded by deleting many journals, including some fannish ones. Many fans started to consider a life beyond LJ. While some did relocate to similar journaling sites, such as InsaneJournal, none of these offered comparable functionality to LJ and the predicted diaspora did not eventuate. The event did lead to the development of Dream-width, which is based on an enhancement of the LJ structure, and which has an upfront commitment to serving the interests of fandom. However, by the time Dreamwidth was established in 2009, there was little motivation for the fandom en masse to move to a site that functionally, if not philosophically, was almost identical to LJ. With the appear-ance on the scene of the very sexy Twitter and Tumblr, a move from LJ to Dreamwidth would have been like buying the same model car in a different colour just after flying skateboards were invented.

## You're like a walking encyclopedia of weirdness. (Dean, 'Roadkill' Season 2, Episode 16)

The *Supernatural* Wiki, known colloquially as the SuperWiki, was started by an Austral-ian fan named Hope in August 2006, who realized that a Wiki model – an example of web 2.0 – fit perfectly with her aim for an inclusive fandom site and had greater potential than a web 1.0-style static website. I started work on the Wiki in 2006, later joined the admin group, and eventually took over running the Wiki in 2009. For me, the SuperWiki encapsulates how social media can serve fandom. It's a place that allows creation and connection and values all works – whether from the show itself or the fans – equally.

The goal of SuperWiki is to provide an extensive information resource and compen-dium of fan knowledge. Similar to Wikipedia, any *Supernatural* fan can add informa-tion to the site, which means the content of the SuperWiki is as incredibly diverse and quirky as the fandom that creates it. A unique feature of the SuperWiki is that it includes entries about the *Supernatural* fandom and our activities alongside that of the show, those who work on it and the many tie-in materials such as novels, comics and anime series. We document what fans create, where we are online, and also offline activities like conventions. The integration of fanworks in the SuperWiki, means that a visit to the entry on Castiel will supply the reader not only with canonical information about the character but also about provide links to fan projects documenting Castiel's hairstyles over the seasons, fanfiction featuring Castiel or people role-playing the angel on Twit-ter. It reflects the diversity of ways in which fans interact with the show.

The Wiki is not only a resource, it is a site for fan creativity in itself. Hundreds of fans have been actively part of the Wiki project. Fans can participate in whatever way interests them; other than having a basic style guide, there are no restrictions on how fans contribute. Some people like to proofread or fact check, some update entries as new episodes air, while others take on particular projects like translating Enochian or documenting the *Star Wars* references. A fan once said to me, 'I love working on the SuperWiki because it's big enough that it feels like I am part of a really important pro-ject and small enough that I feel like my contributions make a difference.' Certainly my own involvement in the SuperWiki took me from a very LiveJournal-centric experience

**Post, Reblog, Follow, Tweet:** *Supernatural* **Fandom and Social Media**
Jules Wilkinson

of fandom into a much broader one as I started visiting other fansites and spaces so I could document them, and also to promote the SuperWiki. I found that people came to work on the SuperWiki from many different corners of fandom. Of particular note was my discovery that there were men in *Supernatural* fandom!

A major aim of the SuperWiki is to increase the accessibility of both the show and the fandom. *Supernatural* is a specifically American narrative, with many of its cultural references reflecting those of its geeky Gen X writers, yet fans of the show span generations and many countries. The SuperWiki episode entries provide fans with information about references they may have missed or not understood – whether it's a demon quoting from a 1960s cartoon series, Dean using the name of the drummer from AC/DC as an alias, or the origins of the 'Bloody Mary' urban legend. Synopses and full transcripts of each episode allow further detailed reading of the text, and possibly elucidate references that subtitles or dubbing of the show in other languages may have obfuscated. The Wiki records definitions for our unique vernacular, helping to explain to newer fans terms that may otherwise act to exclude them from fannish dialogue. Knowing the meaning of mpreg (stories which feature male pregnancy) or Destiel (the term used to designate a romantic relationship between Castiel and Dean) can help avoid some awkward conversations and also help you find the fanart you are looking for. It also provides wonderful insights into the adoption and dissemination of terms over time.

I've had feedback from actors who used the site as reference after landing a role on the show ('just what is a leviathan?') and even from the *Supernatural* writers themselves. In 2012, there were nearly seven million visits to the *Supernatural* Wiki. It is not only an enormous fandom project, but an immensely popular one. Robbie Thompson tweeted that he wrote "Goodbye Stranger" away from the writers' room and his blu-rays of the show, and that the SuperWiki was an "indispensable" resource.

### You guys! You really punked me! I'm totally gonna tweet this one "Hola, mishamigos. J-squared got me good." (Fictional Misha Collins, 'The French Mistake' Season 6, Episode 15)

By mid-2008, a noticeable number of *Supernatural* fans had Twitter accounts. We often translocated our fannish relationships from other sites, and the first presence of *Supernatural* fandom on Twitter was primarily through these pre-established networks. Over time those networks have merged. Twitter brings together fans, not only from different fandom backgrounds, but also from different cultures. Twitter has brought a broader, more casual viewing audience into contact with the core of creative fandom, and with those people who make the show itself. Twitter has also provided a platform for the fandom to come together as a whole, and our fandom has proved an almost unbeatable force when called on to vote for awards such as the People's Choice Awards, even when up against TV series with many more million viewers.

As Twitter has become part of many people's everyday online experience, it has allowed the creation of relationships between actors, the people making the show and fans, without any intervening filter. Actors Misha Collins and later Jared Padalecki were drawcards for many fans to join Twitter. Currently there are over twenty members of the *Supernatural* crew on Twitter, providing fans with previously rare insights into how the show is made and connections with those who make it.

The immediacy of Twitter, combined with the ability to tag tweets with a subject, has been exploited by the *Supernatural* fandom during conventions. Use of a hashtag creates a public forum for discussion of an event. Fans at a convention can tweet in real-time exactly what is happening at an event, like a micro-broadcast. Fansites will compile these tweets to provide a summary of a panel, and of course we link to all of these on the SuperWiki. Social media provides the tools, and fandom makes them work for us. Of course, we don't always use those powers for good.

In the week leading up to the start of *Supernatural*'s Season 5, @SuperWiki started ending tweets with #luciferiscoming as a mischievous way to get attention for the show. In the 24 hours leading up to the premiere of Season 5, the tag started on Twitter. A full blown religious conflagration broke out when musician Sean Combs (@iamdiddy), who has over a million followers and was unaware of the context of #luciferiscoming, started posting with a #Godishere tag in retaliation. Both tags dominated the trending topics list. Eventually Twitter management stepped in, and banned both God and Lucifer from appearing in trending topics. Actor Traci Dinwiddie tweeted after the premiere to say: 'Kripke and all were blown away by the *SPN* fandom's "tweeter take-over"! It was the buzz of the evening! Well done, #Supernatural! Xoxo.'

**Bobby: I asked for a computer.**
**Sam: It is a computer.**
**Bobby: No, a computer has buttons.**
**('Mommie Dearest' Season 6, Episode 19)**
During the same time that Twitter was gaining popularity with fans, so was another microblogging site – Tumblr. Tumblr was the new toy fandom was looking for. In operation since 2007, Tumblr started to gain a significant fandom presence in late 2009, not coincidentally soon after it launched its iPhone app. The syndication of *Supernatural* on TNT in January 2010, captured a new generation of viewers: fans who had grown up with social media and smartphones. Tumblr, where an endless stream of high resolution graphics is available at the swipe of a finger, became the site of choice for these fans, one best viewed on the newly released iPad. Graphics dominate Tumblr, primarily in the form of animated gifs and photosets, often enhanced or altered using Photoshop, which may feature dialogue from the show, or the fan's own text. It can be used to present an episode reaction, character analysis or a piece of silliness or prettiness. The ability to tag posts means a fan can easily search for posts on a topic, although this of course relies on individual fans tagging their posts consistently. If you're

**Post, Reblog, Follow, Tweet: *Supernatural* Fandom and Social Media**
Jules Wilkinson

searching for episode reactions and analysis, it may appear under the episode name #BloodBrother or #ALLTHEWINCHESTERFEELS. Tumblr doesn't require fans to work together for fandom to operate on the site, although fans on Tumblr do cooperate and collaborate on projects. By contrast, LJ relies on a fan-organized infrastructure, with sites such as the *Supernatural Newsletter* essential to help fans find content and run the many creative endeavours there.

Tumblr has become the new home base of much of the *Supernatural* fandom, but in contrast to the early days of the fandom, it is common for fans to participate in fandom on multiple social media sites at once. LiveJournal, along with FanFiction.net, remains the primary place where *Supernatural* fanfiction is created, although an increasing amount is now also being posted on the multifandom *Archive of Our Own.com*, which conveniently allows the downloading of stories in formats compatible with e-readers.

### A bloody, violent monster and you wanna be Facebook friends with him? (Dean, 'Changing Channels' Season 5, Episode 8)

There is no doubt that *Supernatural* is now one of the most active fandoms in the world. By the end of 2012, there had been 56 *Supernatural* conventions held in the United States, Canada, Italy, Brasil, United Kingdom, Spain, Germany, France and Australia. At the 2012 'Jus In Bello Convention' held in Rome, fans from an estimated 46 countries were in attendance. On the *Supernatural* Wiki, we have had visitors from nearly 200 countries. *Supernatural* fandom is more dispersed than it has ever been, but also more connected. If a fan flaps her wings on Tumblr, her feels will be felt around the Internet. The newer social media sites haven't replaced the older ones, but they have changed how they operate. LJ has made changes in recent years to mimic the utility of the newer sites, but it is the existing fannish infrastructure and relationships that keeps fans on LJ, more than the ability to scroll through a friends list or click a button to share a post.

The show itself, which started with a Pilot broadcast on Yahoo, is now available through streaming on Netflix and Hulu. Seven years ago it may have taken hours to download an episode; now a fan in Australia could (hypothetically of course) download and watch the episode on her phone between the time it airs on the East and West Coast in the United States. She can discuss the episode not only with fans from around the world, but with the people who made the show as well. The *Supernatural* fandom has developed along with the social networking sites and new media. Our fandom has capitalized on this infrastructure, and it has facilitated the growth of a dynamic, global fandom that now also encompasses the cast and crew of the show, in what we call the *Supernatural* Family.

### Acknowledgements
Thanks to Simone, Morgan and Luminosity for the beta editing and encouragement, and the whole *Supernatural* fandom for seven years of passion and craziness. ●

GO FURTHER

**Books**

*Some of Us Really Do Watch for the Plot*
Jules Wilkinson and Andie Masino (Eds.)
(Louisville, KY: Café Press, 2007)

**Film/Television**

*Supernatural*, Eric Kripke, creator (Los Angeles:Warner Brothers, 2005–).

'Crossroad Blues', Steve Boyum, dir. *Supernatural* (Los Angeles: Warner Brothers, 2006)

'Season Seven, Time for a Wedding!', Tim Andrew, dir. *Supernatural*
(Los Angeles: Warner Brothers, 2011)

'The Real Ghostbusters', James L. Conway, dir. *Supernatural*
(Los Angeles: Warner Brothers, 2009)

'Roadkill', Charles Beeson, dir. *Supernatural* (Los Angeles: Warner Brothers, 2007)

'The French Mistake', Charles Beeson, dir. *Supernatural*
(Los Angeles: Warner Brothers, 2011)

'Mommie Dearest', John Showalter, dir. *Supernatural*
(Los Angeles: Warner Brothers, 2011)

'Changing Channels', Charles Beeson, dir. *Supernatural*
(Los Angeles: Warner Brothers, 2009)

**Online**

'Do you have any scoop about ...?'
Michael Ausiello
*TV Guide*. 24 January 2007, http://www.tvguide.com/news/scoop-30554.aspx.

Tracy Dinwiddie [Twitter], 11 September 2009, http://twitter.com/GrooveGoddess/
status/3906490289.

**Post, Reblog, Follow, Tweet: *Supernatural* Fandom and Social Media**
Jules Wilkinson

'The WB's 'Supernatural' & Yahoo! Entertainment Give Users an Exclusive Sneak Peek of This Highly Anticipated Fall Series from Warner Bros. Television Productions'. *Futon Critic*, 6 September 2005, http://www.thefutoncritic.com/news.aspx?id=20050906wb01.

'The Top 20 Showrunners to Follow on Twitter'
Lindsay Silberman

*TV Guide*. 28 February 2012, http://www.tvguide.com/News/Top-Showrunners-Follow-Twitter-1044194.aspx.

# 'I THINK DAD WANTS US TO PICK UP WHERE HE LEFT OFF — YOU KNOW, SAVING PEOPLE, HUNTING THINGS. THE FAMILY BUSINESS.'

**DEAN TO SAM IN 'WENDIGO'**
SEASON 1, EPISODE 2

# **Fan Appreciation no.1**
## Ash48: The Vidder

**Interview by Lynn Zubernis**

*Supernatural* has inspired a rich variety of technically impressive fan videos, from humorous 'crack' vids to emotional reflections of canon to 'alternate universe (AU)' vids that tell stories canon has never explored. One of the most prolific and well-known vidders, Sarah House, known within fandom as Ash48, discusses the reasons she's passionate about *Supernatural*, and the story behind some of her most popular vids.

**Lynn Zubernis (LZ):** *What is it about* Supernatural *that makes you want to create fan videos about the show?*

**Ash48:** That's THE question. What exactly is it about *SPN* that makes it so compelling? How can a show, that can be flawed at times, create such an intense passion with so many people? I ask myself that many times. *Supernatural* is still the only show I feel passionate about and connected to in a way that inspires me to vid (or write meta, make picspams, etc.). I love and enjoy many other shows but they don't really inspire me to want to search through hours and hours of footage and extract what I need to make a fanvid.

In a nutshell, the appeal and passion comes down to the characters of Sam and Dean. I have always enjoyed bromance (a big fan of *Starsky & Hutch* [William Frederick Blinn, ABC, 1975-1979], *Simon and Simon* [Philip DeGuere, CBS, 1981-1989] and *The Professionals* [Brian Clemens, ITV, 1977-1983]) so a show featuring brothers working together was something that would appeal to me. It also helps that it's a genre show. I particularly enjoy thrillers, horror, mystery and science fiction so I knew the style of the show would also be something I would like. It doesn't hurt that they are extremely good looking and have amazing on-screen chemistry. They have a powerful and fluctuating dynamic that is fascinating and wonderful to watch. The myth arc (especially the first five years), is intriguing enough to keep me hooked. Even now, as they work through a variety of different seasonal arcs, I am emotionally invested because I have history with the show and I have found a place (fandom) that I love and don't want to give up any time soon.

**LZ:** *What are some of the songs that you've been inspired to vid because of their relevance to SPN?*

**Ash48:** When I heard Johnny Cash's 'Hurt' (2002) I immediately pictured Dean's story and the idea of Dean and the deal. It's probably one of my favourite vids – in terms of a song relating to a character's arc AND it telling the story I wanted to for Dean. It was actually the last verse that really cemented the song for me:

**Fan Appreciation no.1**
Ash48: The Vidder

*Figure 1: 'Hurt'*

> If I could start again
> A million miles away
> I would keep myself
> I would find a way

I am completely fascinated by Dean's decision to sell his soul to bring Sam back. At the end of the vid I wanted to pose the question: if Dean knew the pain and torment he and Sam were going to suffer in the future, would he still make the deal? I am also fascinated by Dean's inner turmoil – this song really spoke to me about that. At the time I made that vid, Dean was drinking a lot and, as I saw it, self-harming. Even though the song was about drug use, I extended it to cover drinking, so it fit Dean.

Dolly Parton's '9 to 5' (1980) is particularly weird choice to vid because it doesn't really have the *SPN feel* about it at all – but I felt the lyrics were perfect for the Winchesters.

> Workin' 9 to 5
> What a way to make a livin'
> Barely gettin' by
> It's all takin'
> And no givin'
> They just use your mind
> And you never get the credit
> It's enough to drive you
> Crazy if you let it

I always see them as working hard and not being rewarded (outside of

*Figure 2: 'No Bravery'*

their own satisfaction of saving people) and the notion of connecting the mundane and normal '9 to 5' job with the job they do rather tickled me. I picked the song and knew I wanted to vid it before I had the idea of using the episode 'It's a Terrible Life' (Season 4, Episode 17). Once I figured out how to use that episode to structure the vid, I was confident I could make it work.

I sat on the song 'No Bravery' (James Blunt, 2006) for ages. It was a song that had the feel I was after but I was concerned about it being too melodramatic and too sentimental. After sitting on it for months, I bit the bullet and just did it. I've always wanted to highlight the plight of the victims in the show, so this song was the perfect vehicle for that. *Supernatural* often shows us children suffering and so these lyrics became a major inspiration for making this vid.

> There are children standing here,
> Arms outstretched into the sky,
> But no one asks the question why,
> He has been here.
> Brothers lie in shallow graves.
> Fathers lost without a trace.
> A nation blind to their disgrace,
> Since he's been here.

I translated 'he' to be a personification of evil.

'Where Do We Draw the Line' is a vid I hold very close to me. Looking back it's probably not as well edited as it could have been, but I remember

**Fan Appreciation no.1**
Ash48: The Vidder

*Figure 3: 'Behind Blue Eyes'*

working really closely with the song and mapping out each visual. I am constantly fascinated by the thin line the boys walk – in what they are prepared to do for each other. This song really spoke to me about how far they'd take it. I remember watching 'All Hell Breaks Loose' (Season 2, Episodes 21-22) and freaking out when Sam was about to hit Jake with the iron bar. It was a line I didn't want Sam to cross. He didn't, and for that he was killed. It's a fabulous conflict. Similarly with Dean making the deal for Sam's life and John making the deal for Dean's. That was the central idea behind this vid.

> What does tomorrow want with me
> What does it matter what I see
> If I can't choose my own design
> Tell me where do we draw the line

'Behind Blue Eyes' (The Who, 1971) is another song I listened to over and over. In my mind it was the perfect Sam song because it talks about what goes on in Sam's troubled mind. It not only reflects what he thinks of himself but what (I thought) fandom was thinking of him at the time.

> No one knows what it's like
> To be the bad man
> To be the sad man
> And no one knows
> What it's like to be hated
> To be fated to telling only lies

The comments I often get are: 'but Sam doesn't have blue eyes.' It's a sure sign that the viewer hasn't understood what I was trying to do with the video. I did take a risk with the interpretation of 'blue' as sad rather than eye colour.

**LZ:** *Your process in creating fanvids is in some ways similar to the process in creating fanfic, including the tension between wanting the fanwork to be well received and wanting to express something that's personal.*

**Ash48:** I imagine the thinking process is much the same. I always have my audience in mind when I make a vid. I think we can say 'I am doing this for myself,' but in reality we're not. Sure, we *enjoy* that creative process and it gives us pleasure, but without an audience I think the experience is incomplete. If something fails we can say 'it's ok because I am doing it for myself' but, personally, that argument stopped working for me early on. There's no doubt I want a vid to be enjoyed, accepted and understood, so the questions I always ask myself relate directly to what the viewer will get out of it. That's not to say that I *only* make vids for an audience. I want to enjoy the finished product as much as I want to enjoy the process. I ask myself 'what do I want to say' and 'what do I want the audience to feel' so I don't lose focus.

**LZ:** *One of the things you identify as a goal in vidding is telling a clear, complex story. How do you accomplish this?*

**Ash48:** This is tricky because I feel I am yet to achieve a vid that *'really achieved a coherent narrative, or told a particularly compelling story'*. Structuring a clear narrative is difficult for me and it's why I don't do AU vids very often. My idea of narrative in a video is the journey it takes from the beginning to the end. If the vid starts with a character in a certain 'place' (frame of mind, situation, etc.) and ends with them in another 'place', then I consider the vid to have a narrative structure. With that in mind, the ones that I think came close would be 'Hurt' and 'Wrong'. 'Hurt' had a distinctive ending (Dean reflecting on his decision to sell his soul) and therefore I think the vid had a narrative flow to get to that point (that was my aim anyway). 'Wrong' started by telling three separate character stories and ended with all three coming together to show how each of their stories (or individual battles) helped them fight together as Team Free Will.

The other style of narrative is when I specifically set out to tell a story.

**Fan Appreciation no.1**
Ash48: The Vidder

*Figure 4: 'Wrong'*

I have only ever attempted that twice – 'Violence and Sex' and 'Winter-song'. 'Violence and Sex' was a massive challenge as I attempted to tell a distinct AU narrative (for the first time). The biggest difficulty was creating a moment at the end that showed Sam 'taming' Dean by fighting back and them then coming together without Dean having to use violence to sublimate his sexual desire for Sam. This vid specifically told an AU narrative of Dean wanting Sam sexually and not being able to act on it, so he used violence as a way of both controlling his desires and actually touching Sam. Sam took and accepted it but in the end he fought back and Dean discovered that Sam wanted him just as much (see … fanfic! If I could write this story I would!).

**LZ:** *How do you manipulate the existing visuals of the show to emphasize what you want to convey?*

**Ash48:** I consider myself a fairly 'simple' vidder. I don't use special effects very often, I rely on simple techniques to emphasize or show specific elements in the story. The thing I probably use the most is either black and white or desaturated shots to indicate a memory, flashback or inner thoughts. I also use a vignette to show the character either dreaming or thinking. I use colour to emphasize a mood or to indicate how a character is feeling. In the recent vid 'Wintersong', I decided to desaturate Dean's present/current place because I wanted to create a feeling of him being sombre, lacking 'life' and vibrancy. His memories of Sam are highly saturated so the viewer got the impression that his memories are vivid and much happier.

I learned fairly early on not to use effects just because they are in the

Figure 5: 'Supernatural At
The Movies'

programme and look 'cool'. They have to mean something. Perspective is always interesting and can be one of the biggest challenges. If I am making a vid from Dean's POV, for example, I always check that what we are seeing is something Dean has actually seen (or knows about) and we always have to see clips of the character so we are reminded through whose eyes we are seeing this. Sometimes there's no character's POV but rather just me (and ultimately the audience) – the gag reels and a lot of my celebratory or crack vids fall into this category.

Transitions are powerful ways to affect the mood of the viewer or to link visuals. Fades are particularly effective when trying to create poignancy (my long-time beta reviewer, Steph, gave me some great insight on incorporating moments of black in a vid to indicate separation from one moment to the next or to emphasize an emotion or powerful moment). The cross-dissolve is probably my most used transition. I particularly love it if one clip contextually matches the next (Sam giving Dean the amulet and Dean discarding the amulet, for example) – a cross-dissolve will enhance that connection. It's also a great way to show what a character is thinking. The song will usually dictate which style of transitions to use. Fast songs are usually just good old fashioned plain cuts (my fave!), slower songs lend themselves to lovely long cross-dissolves and fades.

**LZ:** *What sort of visual elements inspire you?*

**Ash48:** *Supernatural*'s cinematography is stunning. They give vidders some lovely footage to work with. We are fortunate because a lot of the imagery is symbolic and thus can be used in a number of contexts. For example, the image of Dean fighting his way out of his grave in 'Lazarus

**Fan Appreciation no.1**
Ash48: The Vidder

Rising' (Season 4, Episode 1). It can be seen as representing Dean's inner struggle (escaping an inner darkness) or symbolic of Dean's continual fight. I particularly love the moment when the camera pulls up to reveal the circle of fallen trees. Whenever I see that I think of the contrasting moment when the camera zooms into his eye after he dies in 'No Rest for the Wicked' (Season 3, Episode 16). The patterns are the same. A circle surrounded by up radiating lines. I have used these two shots together because of the way they match and also to show Dean's death and subsequent rebirth. In 'At the Movies – the Sequel' I did an 'arthouse' segment that purely matched circular images in the show.

The gorgeous outdoor scenes are wonderful to use when representing the boys against the world or trying to create a feeling of contentment between them (as I did in 'Wintersong').

Another iconic visual is the coffee cup falling from Sam's grasp when he sees John lying on the floor in the hospital. I used this visual a number of times in my early vids because it looks gorgeous and because it's become symbolic of loss. I haven't done it yet, but I would love to marry that shot with the glass of milk falling when young!Bobby knocked it over in 'At Death's Door'. I am sure that moment was a call back to John's death. Connecting John and Bobby's deaths like that is awesome and what makes the show so special.

The shots of the Impala on the road are fabulous for symbolizing Sam and Dean's 'journey'. They make great motifs or symbolic scene transitions. It enhances a vid's message to use iconic or powerful scenes as a motif. I remember learning about the use of motifs in film during film crit classes. They are a great way to show the progression of a narrative or character's story line if an image can be repeated three times throughout the vid (or film). They can also work as an anchor for the viewer – bringing them back to the central idea the vidder is trying to get across. An example would be my use of external footage in 'Wrong'. It connected the individual storylines and (in my mind) brought the viewer back to the notion that there's an outside world that is being affected by these three characters' actions.

**LZ:** *You've done a little work with AU vids and included manips (photo manipulations) to tell a story that's outside canon. Is the process of making an AU vid different?*

**Ash48:** I find AU vid-making really hard. The biggest problem for me is looking at the footage outside of its context. For example, when Dean is at the crossroads selling his soul, I can only ever see that footage knowing what went before and came after. In an AU vid, that moment could be anything. He could be meeting a secret lover, hitching a ride, hunting for a monster. For an AU vid to work, the vidder has to 'sell' the idea that what the character is doing in that moment isn't what they were doing in the show. It's tricky. I think the process is different because the thinking is different. Telling an existing story is easier because the footage is already there, it's just a matter of arranging it the best way possible to get your message across. With an AU vid the thinking has to extend to – how am I going to sell this? How can I convince the audience that this is what happened? How can I manipulate the footage to the best effect? AU vidding is about telling a *new* story. Doing a character study, episode recap or celebration-style vid is telling (or showing) an existing story, with the added 'comment' by the vidder. For example, something like 'Smile Like You Mean It' is taking something that exists and condensing it into 1 minute to give us more information about a moment that went for mere seconds on the screen.

**LZ:** *Vidders have described a variety of motivations for vidding, from celebration to escapism, to meta and social critique. What do you see as your motivation?*

**Ash48:** The question of motivation is fascinating to me. I often wonder what drives me to spend hours and hours working on a vid. A lot comes down to the addictive nature of editing – I love the process so much. It's immensely satisfying laying down clips and finding the best way to make them work. It's also frustrating, but I think that's part of the 'addiction'. It's like working on a huge jigsaw puzzle – a process of trial and error. It's frustrating when you can't find the right piece but when you do there's a wonderful feeling of satisfaction and achievement. While I'm making a vid I'm usually in a 'happy' place. It's hard to explain but I'm usually more positive when I'm vidding. So in that respect it *is* a type of escapism. My moods can sometimes directly relate to how well a vid is coming along (I used to think this was strange until Luminosity described the same thing happens to her). There's also the knowledge that I will be sharing the finished work at the end. That usually excites me and motivates me to keep going.

I have great admiration for vidders who can provide a social commentary in their vids. 'Women's Work' (Luminosity and Sisabet) has to be one of my all-time favourite vids for making a comment on how the show uses women. For me, I just haven't been motivated in that direction (yet!). I haven't felt passionate enough about a social issue to make me want to vid about it.

Another major source of motivation is working on vids for other people. I have put myself up for auction a few times (fandomaid) and I find working on a vid that someone else has either provided the idea or the song for is very motivating. I love the challenge of working with something I haven't thought of. There's something intrinsically rewarding about knowing you're making it for someone in particular (and you know at least one person will watch it!). It's also a great way to connect with fellow fans. Counteragent and I got to know each other after I made her requested Bobby vid ('Mr. Sandman'). I wanted to make a Bobby vid but lacked inspiration and motivation – until I was *required* to make one. It got me moving and I was really pleased with the result. Counteragent was pleased (and so was Jim Beaver! Yay!). And there's no doubt that someone paying money (to a charity) to have you make a vid for them is ego-boosting.

**LZ:** *Some vids seem to be purely celebratory – it feels like we (fandom) are all celebrating our show together.*

**Ash48:** Absolutely! This is definitely about me sharing my love for the show with people I know love it too. Being active in the *Supernatural* fandom means I read a lot and I see what concerns and interests fans. In that respect, I don't work in a vacuum. I try to bring things that fans are talking about into my vids so there's a connection – a connection between my vid and the fan experience, and between my fan experience and others' experience. For example, 'Woo Hoo' is taking moments from the show that are easily identifiable as 'great' moments. Moments we all recognize as being quintessentially 'Supernatural'. I make these because I like to build excitement for myself and then share that excitement.

**LZ:** *Other vids seem to be analogous to 'fix it fic', working through things in canon that have been painful for fans or difficult to make sense of.*

**Ash48:** Yes, very much so. Often I am struck by an idea like, 'Sam really wasn't saved after all. Sure, he survived but he still suffered tremendously.' I then have the urge to explore that, so I make a vid like 'Maybe I Could Be Saved'. As I mentioned earlier, I also have the audience in mind. So with that one I thought it might be good to share my realization with everyone else. I think the power of vidding (and the visual medium) is being able to rearrange the footage to tie moments from earlier episodes to later ones. It's a way of writing meta in a visual way. For example, in Season 1 Sam leaves Dean to look for Dad ('Scarecrow' Episode 11). In Season 2, he leaves Dean to find answers about himself ('Hunted' Episode 10). He later leaves Dean because he feels out of control in 'Good God Y'All' (Season 5, Episode 2). The theme of leaving continues into Season 7 when Sam leaves Dean because Dean betrayed his trust. All these moments can be brought together visually to tell that story and make a comment about how Sam uses this method of coping.

Character study vids work in the same way. Sam and Dean are complex characters. They have many layers. I am always trying to find reasons for their behaviours – and look for threads from past events that explain current behaviours. The same way a writer can give us a character's inner thoughts (and therefore insight to their actions), a vidder can visually make those connections and give the viewer new insights (hopefully). I think it also allows a vidder to share their experience of the show. In 'Hurt' I was telling the audience that *I* see Dean as selfharming when he drinks. In 'Behind Blue Eyes', my personal comment is that Sam isn't understood. In the *SPN* 'verse Sam believes he isn't understood, and I think fans are often unfair *to* Sam because they don't really understand him.

**LZ:** *Then there are the vids that express the things we celebrate in fandom, but don't necessarily talk about openly outside fandom – that is, we don't JUST watch for the plot, we also like to LOOK. In a sense these are celebratory – celebrating the boys' hotness – and in a sense they have a little bit of social critique in them too, as fans both assert our right to objectify*

Figure 6: '*I Like The Way You Move*'

**Fan Appreciation no.1**
Ash48: The Vidder

*and simultaneously question it.*

**Ash48:** Yes! 'Looking' is very much part of the experience. I am always up front about my love of looking (some may say drooling). There's no denying part of the fan experience is sharing our love for the way the boys look. It's not only a celebration of *them* but also celebrating the fact that someone else thinks the same way you do – that they like and appreciate how drop dead gorgeous they are. Maybe it's when they are smiling, maybe it's when they are covered in blood. I haven't been overt in my social comment about our want (need?) to look (perv …) but I think by putting such videos into the public domain we are putting that comment out there. I admit I have questioned myself when making some of the more obvious objectifying vids. Particularly 'I Like The Way You Move' and 'I'm a Lucky Man'. As these focus on a real person, I am more aware of the nature of the vid. I even sent the first one to an online friend and said 'Am I overstepping the mark here? Am I being a creepy fangirl?' She answered that there was a level of respect and a sense of celebration so not to worry. Making vids like that is my way of celebrating a person that I appreciate and admire. I know that others feel the same so I know there will be an audience. And, like any other vid I make, it's showing others how *I* see this person. (It's one vid that I often go to when I'm feeling down. It's my personal happy-making vid.)

**LZ:** *Some of your vids are slash – either Wincest AU or celebrating the 'epic love' of Jared and Jensen (J2). What is the motivation behind these vids?*

**Ash48:** I enjoy Wincest and I find it easy to believe it exists because of the nature of the show. I love it when they give us moments that help support the idea. I am also acutely aware that many don't like the idea of Wincest, so I am mindful when I make a vid that it can appeal to both types of audiences. The only 'real' Wincest vids I have made are 'Violence and Sex' and 'Wintersong'. These are the only vids I have gone into manipping footage to really sell the idea. The show provides so much footage that is easy to manipulate the footage into telling a Wincest AU. It's more about rearranging the footage, slowing it down or merging two clips to emphasize a sexual intent between the boys.

All the other vids focus on the bromance – my number one favourite thing about the show. However, as with the show, they can be interpreted as Wincest if the viewer chooses to watch it that way. When I made '500

Figure 7: 'Channel Surfing'

Miles' I really hadn't considered it to be Wincest at all (one of my very early vids and I was just becoming aware of Wincest in a major way). It wasn't until someone commented and said 'This is my favourite Wincest vid' that I realized that (of course!) it had been inferred. I mean, with lyrics like 'when I wake up next to you' – it's pretty clear. Mostly I subscribe to the Epic Love Story of Sam and Dean. That's canon and that's what motivates a lot of my bromantic-style vids. I like to *show* the audience just how damn epic their love is. Also, it's my way of *reminding* myself (and fans) that it (still) exists. When the boys are at odds with each other on the show, I use vidding as a type of therapy for getting through the rough spots.

**LZ:** *There are a few vids that are critique or commentary on the show and the reciprocal relationship between fans and the actors/producers. What inspired these vids?*

Figure 8: 'Channel Hopping'

**Fan Appreciation no.1**
Ash48: The Vidder

*Figure 9: 'Love Shack'*

**Ash48:** I am often inspired by things outside of the show – the fan campaign to send thousands of rubber ducks to the set, the winning of awards, etc. 'Soapernatural' was my way of dealing with the utter frustration I was feeling during the first half of Season 8 with all the 'soapy' elements in the show. I have always had an interest in the various genres the show covers, so I felt like it was in my 'style' to produce a vid like this. It's almost a mockery of my past genre-study vids ('Channel Hopping', 'Channel Surfing' and 'At the Movies I and II') and a comment on the direction I saw the show taking. I admit that it was one vid that I actually hoped The Powers That Be would see so they knew how (some) fans were observing it.

'They Did What ...?' was made out of frustration also, when the network cancelled a much-anticipated broadcast. Looking back, it may well have been overreacting (!!), but in some ways it was a breakthrough for me because I'd never made this type of 'commentary' vid before. The style was also different for me and I ended up being pleased with its structure more than anything.

'Ducks', 'Stupornatural' and 'The Meta Song' were celebrations of other fanworks and efforts. I get very inspired by what other people do. When I saw 'Stupornatural' I was blown away by the film-makers' efforts and had to celebrate that. The same with 'The Meta Song'. A 15-year-old fangirl wrote that song and I wanted to put visuals to it for her. I'm currently assisting another fan (Counteragent) in editing her original *SPN* film. Not only am I loving the process of editing original footage, but the collaboration is fantastic! I feel like I am part of something significant and we are sharing a common goal. A lot of fans are involved in this project and I think when it is realized it will be an amazing example of what can be achieved when fans come together.

**LZ:** *Finally, there are the 'crack vids', which are technically amazing and absolutely hilarious. What's the motivation for those?*

**Ash48:** These are among my favourites. Not only because they were tremendous fun to work on, but they were also well received and there's no denying that there is a certain amount of satisfaction in that. The reaction that 'Channel Hopping' received completely blew me way. It came as a huge surprise and provided the motivation for many of the future 'crack' vids. There's no doubt I am motivated by knowing I have made people laugh. I think if we can share a laugh then we are doing what we enjoy in fandom – and that's to have fun. I also like not taking myself too seriously. I like it if I can find a way to make observations that are considered 'crack-ish'. Laughing at ourselves (and the show) can help put things into perspective. I know I take it all too seriously sometimes. I can get so caught up in the angst of the show and the direction it is taking that I forget that I'm in this for fun. So the crack vids are a way of pulling myself out of that.

I am also motivated by the opportunity to work with talented fans like maichan; 'Channel Hopping' was initially inspired by her early crack vids. I told her in a private e-mail that I had made 'Channel Hopping' after being shown a vid she had made that opened my eyes to the potential of vidding. It was like a huge door opening and I felt like I had discovered a way of vidding that excited me. I was worried that she'd see it as copying but she said she was happy something she had made was inspiring.

~~~~~~~~~~

**GO FURTHER**

**Film/Television**

*Supernatural*, Eric Kripke, creator (Los Angeles: Warner Brothers, 2005–).

'All Hell Breaks Loose', Robert Singer dir. *Supernatural* (Los Angeles: Warner Brothers, 2007)

'Lazarus Rising', Kim Manners dir. *Supernatural* (Los Angeles: Warner Brothers, 2008)

'No Rest for the Wicked', Kim Manners dir. *Supernatural* (Los Angeles: Warner Brothers, 2008)

'Scarecrow', Kim Manners dir. *Supernatural* (Los Angeles: Warner Brothers, 2006)

'Hunted', Rachel Talalay dir. *Supernatural* (Los Angeles: Warner Brothers, 2007)

## Fan Appreciation no.1
### Ash48: The Vidder

'Good God Y'All', Philip Sgriccia dir. *Supernatural* (Los Angeles: Warner Brothers, 2009)

**Online/ Videos**

'9 to 5' [YouTube] 3 October 2009
http://www.youtube.com/watch?v=pQnf81dQr9U

'500 Miles' [YouTube]11 September 2008
http://www.youtube.com/watch?v=AK2yRsXSBJA

'Behind Blue Eyes' [YouTube] 25 January 2010 http://www.youtube.com/
watch?v=xlfFyyLkc_c

'Channel Hopping'[YouTube] 10 May 2008
http://www.youtube.com/watch?v=FzQPbleK-GM

'Dueling Winchesters'[YouTube] 6 April 2012
http://www.youtube.com/watch?v=pi8tmTm_-P8

'Hair' [YouTube] 26 February 2010
http://www.youtube.com/watch?v=13Vhi1ghjil

'His Wings' [YouTube] 22 August 2008
http://www.youtube.com/watch?v=RnveadbnL18

'Hugs' [YouTube] 14 April 2010
http://www.youtube.com/watch?v=D28V7rg1vZc

'Hurt' [YouTube] 12 October 2009
http://www.youtube.com/watch?v=eLLRjwWyRaM

'I Like The Way You Move' [YouTube] 3 September 2011
http://www.youtube.com/watch?v=rjGZSftwXUY

'I'm a Lucky Man' [YouTube] 15 August 2012
http://www.youtube.com/watch?v=rsa6kV-Zock

'I'm Too Sexy' [YouTube] 22 August 2008
http://www.youtube.com/watch?v=3sTffDvolHc

'It's Raining Men' [YouTube] 11 September 2011
http://www.youtube.com/watch?v=Vru77gPtGMg

'Love Shack' [YouTube] 22 July 2010
http://www.youtube.com/watch?v=afFPVITm3Xk

'Maybe I Could Be Saved' [YouTube] 30 May 2012

http://www.youtube.com/watch?v=LTAG9N1vteE

'Mr. Boombastic' [YouTube] 4 November 2010
http://www.youtube.com/watch?v=pwvzHP037xc
'Mr. Sandman' [YouTube] 26 March 2011
http://www.youtube.com/watch?v=xJ5n1uPdn44

'No Bravery' [YouTube] 17 January 2011
http://www.youtube.com/watch?v=-Hg8JK1c-OE

'Our Time is Running Out'[YouTube] 26 November 2007
http://www.youtube.com/watch?v=qHJg1TfpAG8

'Passion In My Pants' [YouTube] 25 September 2012
http://www.youtube.com/watch?v=mB_8Lchu35A

'Set Me Free' [YouTube] 4 October 2010
http://www.youtube.com/watch?v=_-cM57fZQeE

'Shakin' That Ass '[YouTube] 23 April 2007
http://www.youtube.com/watch?v=OvL19RwHe_E

'Smile Like You Mean It' [YouTube] 17 February, 2012 http://www.youtube.com/
watch?v=jpdPxuyNzPQ

'Soapernatural' [YouTube] 11 December 2012
http://www.youtube.com/watch?v=tWJIawjGRI4

'Stupornatural' [YouTube] 22 November 2009
http://www.youtube.com/watch?v=DKwAUpmnrrc

'Sunshine Day' [YouTube] 3 June 2012
http://www.youtube.com/watch?v=q1QbAIR3S6A

'Supernatural at the Movies – The Sequel' [YouTube] 17 May 2011
http://www.youtube.com/watch?v=N8VN29cty5A

'Take Me To The Hospital' [YouTube] 7 February 2008 http://www.youtube.com/
watch?v=jVaSAAsw8uQ

'They Did What?' [YouTube] 29 January 2011
http://www.youtube.com/watch?v=rdo9oWWvHws

'The Look Of Love' [YouTube] 20 April 2009
http://www.youtube.com/watch?v=FWlzDXx49bs

'The Meta Song' [YouTube] 5 March 2011
http://www.youtube.com/watch?v=lo5LQm9_00c

**Fan Appreciation no.1**
Ash48: The Vidder

'Violence And Sex' 1 April 2009
http://ash48.livejournal.com/26666.html

'Walking On Sunshine' [YouTube] 24 August 2009
http://www.youtube.com/watch?v=--WX5cpOh4A

'We Are The Champions' [YouTube] 12 January 2012
http://www.youtube.com/watch?v=1pGWdGqVRZk

'We Will Rock You Rock You' [YouTube] 30 September 2012
http://www.youtube.com/watch?v=YBXPsJz7W2c

'What The Duck' [YouTube] 30 November 2011
http://www.youtube.com/watch?v=5f7RZAtVO6Q

'When The Levee Breaks Levee Breaks' [YouTube] 10 September 2010
http://www.youtube.com/watch?v=YkJzElt_iFA

'Where Do We Draw The Line' [YouTube] 27 January 2009
http://www.youtube.com/watch?v=B_3U35f6Ny8

'Wintersong' [YouTube] 2 December 2012
http://www.youtube.com/watch?v=IquuP0tWU4O

'Women's Work' (Luminosity and Sisabet), 8 April, 2009
http://www.politicalremixvideo.com/2009/04/08/womens-work/

'Woohoo Woohoo' [YouTube] 25 January 2011
http://www.youtube.com/watch?v=CgoVuxvMAI8

'World Spins Madly On' [YouTube] 6 August 2011
http://www.youtube.com/watch?v=jRqfOCtmGVE

'Wrong' [YouTube] 2 December 2010
http://www.youtube.com/watch?v=K320kAPd28s

# 'WE'VE GOT WORK TO DO.'

**SAM TO DEAN IN 'PILOT', AND DEAN TO SAM, IN 'ALL HELL BREAKS LOOSE' PART TWO**
SEASON 1, EPISODE 1 AND SEASON 2, EPISODE 22

Chapter
5

# Family Don't End With Blood: Building the *Supernatural* Family

Mary Frances Casper

→ *Supernatural* was introduced to American audiences in 2005. The handsome young men fighting evil while searching for their father quickly gained fans and followers over the next seven years. The Winchesters became the sons, brothers and fantasy love interests of men and women across the world. Fans were encouraged to develop personal connections with the cast. Knowing that television series live and die by viewership and ratings, audience interaction and fan culture was encouraged from *Supernatural's* inception. IMDb reports that

> Early on in the series, Dean's cell number is given, and for a while the studio had it set up so that anyone dialing the number would hear Jensen Ackles reading the message: 'This is Dean Winchester. If this is an emergency, leave a message. If you are calling about 11-2-83, page me with your coordinates.' The number is 1-866-907-3235.

So began the inclusion of fans into the lives of characters, and the characters into the lives of the fans. Now in its eighth season, *Supernatural* has built a passionate fan base still encouraged to interact with the cast and crew, now through social media (Bement 2012). The *Supernatural* Family (*SPN* Family) fandom has become a force to be reckoned with. While it's difficult to measure the actual size of the *Supernatural* fan base, its impact is evident. Fanfiction, fanart, fansites, YouTube videos, television and media forums, convention attendance and fundraising efforts for causes championed by the *Supernatural* cast demonstrate the prolific nature of the fans and provide a view into the language and traditions of the mythic *Supernatural* Family.

Families develop their own languages based on shared experiences and storytelling. Such stories help family members maintain connections, even when separated by distance, age or circumstance. Over time, the retelling of family stories creates mythic narratives that illustrate the family's history, values, legends and personalities. In a similar fashion, *Supernatural* fans enact their membership in the *Supernatural* Family through quoted dialogue, story extension and fantasy chain scenarios using a myriad of formats: Wiki sites, websites, fanfiction, fanart, fan videos and participation in contests and conventions. This chapter examines the mythic *Supernatural* Family as revealed through fansites, social media, user-generated content, and conventions. Because fan user names are self-selected and used in public forums, both they and the media outlets where they are used, are disclosed. As it is difficult to determine who members actually are, gender is assumed based on the user name and then used in discussion.

**From fan culture to family**

Fan cultures typically develop around books, television and films, and often focus on characters or celebrities. Fandoms (specific fan subcultures) develop language and vernaculars, name themselves and their subgroups, create social structures and determine accepted, expected behaviours that reflect their shared values and meanings. Cultural assumptions are revealed through values, myths and understandings embedded in a fandom's language and stories (Collier, 2005, Downes, 1996, Gauntlett and Hill, 1999, Geertz, 1973). Early members shape a fandom's distinct personality, which then grows and evolves as new members join.

The *Supernatural* Family exemplifies how storytelling creates cultural myths, which then become part of the fandom's culture and identity. Myth is, in essence, a pool of beliefs and interpretations that create and bind unique cultures (Casper, 2007). Myths are shared through stories about the experiences and histories of supernatural or larger-

**Family Don't End With Blood: Building the *Supernatural* Family**
Mary Frances Casper

than-life personages (O'Flaherty, 1988); in this case the Winchesters, using language that gives 'meaning and value to life' (Eliade, 1963, p. 2). As these stories are passed down, signs and their associated meanings build and identify communities by ordering facts and ideas (Barthes, 1972, Leeming, 2004). They become ways to demonstrate family membership, to indicate belonging, and to express family identity. The stories take on a life of their own, creating a family narrative that exists independent of the programme that inspired it. Outsiders may grasp the meanings present in family narratives, but lack the cultural experience to embrace them or see them as 'natural'.

Conversational references to 'show' dialogue and inside jokes about the cast and crew reflect *Supernatural* Family culture and add to the family narrative. The most benign references can cue emotional responses and communicate meanings only fans understand. For example, members posting 'Happy pig n a poke day :)' (mrs_jarpad) and 'Every single Tuesday I listen to "Heat of the moment" by Asia' (notrobinanymore, 2012) are referring to the 'Mystery Spot' (Season 3, Episode 11) in which Dean is killed and Sam is unable to save him over an endless succession of the same Tuesday. Non-'Family' members might read these as cheerful, if confusing, posts, but Family members recognize the underlying love, loss, frustration, anger and loyalty. For Family members, these posts are declarations of shared history and belonging.

## The *Supernatural* Family

While there have been *Supernatural* fan groups since the show began, they officially became family when Jared Padalecki (Sam Winchester) described fans as 'like my third family. I have my family, my on-set family, and then our 'Supernatural' family [...] My 'Supernatural' family's the biggest and strongest, so I love 'em' (MacKenzie, 2011). The name and idea caught on, further establishing the fandom's Winchester-flavoured inclusive, supportive identity.

[t]he fans of *Supernatural* (or, *SPN*, as it is affectionately referred to) are one big dysfunctionally happy family. In fact, that's how an *SPN* fan refers to the friends they have met through the *SPN* fandom, whether in person or online only: The *SPN* Family. This family, born out of a belief that family doesn't end in blood. (Pitt, 2012)

*Supernatural* fans are a tight bunch. The family welcomes new members and guides their behaviour across platforms primarily by adopting Winchester family values and attitudes. As in any extended family there are rebels and outliers, there are matriarchs and patriarchs holding members accountable, and there is a sense of belonging to something larger than you. In 'No Rest For the Wicked' (Season 3, Episode 16), character Bobby Singer tells the Winchester boys that 'family don't end with blood' a motto embraced by the *Supernatural* fandom. The Winchesters love one another, but they don't always like one another, they don't always agree, and they don't always do the right thing. In the

Winchester world, that just means that you love your brother harder, rein him in, teach him right and make him clean up his mess. And if you don't like that, you suck it up. As Bobby tells Dean in 'Lucifer Rising' (Season 4, Episode 1), 'Are you under the impression that family's supposed to make you feel good, make you an apple pie, maybe? They're supposed to make you miserable! That's why they're family!'

It's this unshakeable commitment to family, regardless of circumstance, that reso-nates with fans and creates the fandom's underlying personality.

The heart of the show, and the way in which it most actively offers a response to post-modern cynicism and malaise, lies in *Supernatural*'s advocacy of family and familial bonds as a refuge against the monsters of the darkness, a refuge that has been eagerly welcomed by viewers in the large and active fan community. (Noone, 2010)

In seeking to recreate the Winchester family dynamic, *Supernatural* fans have cre-ated a foundation of support for one another. They will call you on your crap, but they always have your back.

### *Supernatural* Family, Winchester family values

The Winchesters' lives are based on 'saving people, hunting things. You know, the family business'. They counter the tragedy in their own lives by helping others and 'killing as many evil sons-of-bitches' as they possibly can ('Wendigo' Season 1, Episode 2). They defend the defenseless and protect the innocent without asking for or expecting any-thing in return. They put what is right before what is legal and see lying as a conditional offense, while promises must be upheld at any cost. They don't follow any particular religion or attend church, they lie, they cheat and they steal. Yet they are moral men.

The *SPN* Family reflects the values expressed in the programme through the stories they share. Narratives of family belonging, taking care of their own, fighting the good fight, unity and strength, and unwavering loyalty create a mythic Winchester-esque dynamic. Being part of the Family opens the door to a life where 'what would a Winchester do?' seems the unspoken motto.

We are family

Fans proudly identify themselves as part of the *SPN* Family. Sololilia demonstrates how embedded *Supernatural* has become in her life by sharing 'Life's never easy for a Supernatural fan's mom, when the lights go out Mom goes nuts to find 2 things…A freaking candle. her [sic] jar of salt! *True Story Guys*'. Many fans express their love and commitment to the show, some more passionately than others. Allthechickflick-moments defends obsession with *Supernatural* by telling his friend that it's a religion, stating '*Some believe in God, we believe in Kripke.*' Invisiblecake shares 'I'd just like to

**Family Don't End With Blood: Building the *Supernatural* Family**
Mary Frances Casper

——

*Figure 1: The Roadhouse*

say how proud I am to be a part of this fandom/family...I love all of you so much...I just needed to put that out there' and includes an image of the Roadhouse Bar from the show, captioned 'I love everyone in this bar'.

Even close-knit families have disagreements within their ranks. Just as family members who get out of line are rebuked, *SPN* fans call one another to task over online postings. One fan took a screenshot of a Twitter feed argument about removing a character from the show, including the names of the posters, and shared it on her Tumblr page with the comment 'I'm sorry, but this is a family last I checked. I will not stand for this' and tagged it 'if you're gonna hate go somewhere I can't see you' (invisiblecakes, 2012). Another advises fans to remember the importance of family and 'just put the ship wars, the hate, and the arguments away, and remember all we've done for one another, and how much we love each other...' (hunterinabrowncoat, 2012). Vannadear sums it up, saying '*Supernatural* is so much more than a TV show, it's a true family. We may fight all the time over who the favorite is, and meddle in their love lives too often, but we're still the best damn family I've ever had.'

We take care of our own

The *SPN* Family is fiercely loyal to the show and to one another. The fandom is known for mobilizing behind causes championed by the cast and crew, and in support of fellow *SPN* Family members. Scriingankhsandstars expresses awe over the love of the *Supernatural* Family:

My first real experience was watching the absolute amazingness that is the *SPN* Family coming together for something and someone they love; Jared and Gen Padalecki. When the couple announced their pregnancy, the Family went crazy raising money for St. Judes. Soon after that was the People's Choice Awards. TWO awards were won for *Supernatural* because of the dedication of the fans.

Fan testimonials which describe helping fans battling cancer, depression and emotional turmoil barely scratch the surface of the love and support provided by the *SPN* Family. As scriingankhsandstars goes on to share:

My biggest supporters [...] have made it clear that I am the same to them as they are to me; Family. Thank you to those of you who have been helping me fight my most recent demons [...] It's nice to have backup when I need it. I love you all dearly and couldn't imagine my life without you, all of you. My Supernatural Family is perfect.

Not only does this post provide a blueprint of expected behaviours, it is laced with show vernacular equating the fan's experience with that of the Winchesters.

*SPN* Family members often use social media to keep each other informed of contests, events and issues. When a photograph of Jared and Genevieve Padalecki's son was released without their consent, fans quickly spread the word. 'The photo of Gen Jared and little baby Thomas was stolen. And Jared was upset about it. Please if you have it posted please remove it. ~Lis'. When rosettaslair discovered that a fellow fan was seriously ill she called on the Family for help, reporting that Sashi:

> has a serious disease and isn't able to work or pay for a very expensive surgery she needs. If she doesn't get it, she will die. I simply cannot sit back and watch it happen. As a fandom, more than that, as the *Supernatural* family, we need to do all we can to help her. If you can't donate, spread the world. Let's help her get her medical treatment!

The post included a link to contact Sashi with moral support, and another to make donations. Though rosettaslair and Sashi had never spoken, rosettaslair felt that she knew Sashi from reading her posts and was compelled to take action on behalf of a fellow Family member.

Keeping up with extended family can be difficult, so fans use social media to share their own and *SPN* Family stories. Hunterinabrowncoat calls for a video reminiscent of a family Christmas letter, which recognizes what...

> [...] the show and the fandom has done: the lives it's saved, the stories of people fighting their demons because Sam and Dean did, helping people move on from terrible losses, the fandom raising money for people in need (like managing to pay for someone's life-saving surgery!), and raising over $40,000 when Thomas was born ... all that amazing stuff, to remind us of how we're a family, no matter what.

The post goes on to suggest sending the video to the *Supernatural* cast to remind them of what they, and the *SPN* Family, have accomplished. Ccaastiel provides what could be the Family creed: '*Supernatural* Fandom. No matter what happens. No matter who dies. We will stick by together until the very end and kick whatever happens in the motherfucking ASSBUTT'.

## Fight the good fight

The *SPN* Family mobilizes to support causes championed by the cast and crew of the programme. Fan generosity and participation has become part of the Family mythology. The expectation of fan support is implicit in Hurricane Sandy relief appeals to 'a worldwide fandom with a huge heart' asking for donations on behalf of the *SPN* Family to the American Red Cross because 'we cannot think of a more appropriate organization for the *SPN* family to support' (*Winchester Bros.com*). Fans are rewarded for being part of the *SPN* Family mission. As rosettaslair shares

> Being a part of the supernatural family makes me want to cry sometimes [...] I'm just happy and very emotional about what we all accomplished today [...] I believe each one of us is making a difference right now and [...] It's just perfection *choking up* Thanks, you kind souls! We are changing lives and it's one of the things that make this fandom a family! <3

Fans share their progress and celebrate their efforts with one another, both reaffirming the desirability of membership and reinforcing what it means to be part of the *SPN* Family.

## Together we are mighty

As one fan reports, 'I feel like we can do absolutely anything we set our minds to if we're together' (invisiblecakes, 2012). Embedded within the good fight commentary is the idea that it's the *SPN* Family against the world, just as it's the Winchesters against the world. The limited viewership size is a point of pride with *SPN* Family members, who see themselves as special – the ones in the know. As Far Away Eyes says on *The Winchester Family Business.com*,

> It is amazing what this "little show that could" can do to us, no? ... When they call us the *Supernatural* Family, I believe it. We are that. It's amazing how much good we can do through a collective effort for charity.

Vannadear crows,

> How many other shows' fans can say they've accomplished even half as much as we have? Charities, Online Polls, Random acts of Kindness, GISHWHES? Our ratings may be under 2 million, but we are still so fucking mighty! Because we do the impossible, time and time again.

Not all of that power is used altruistically. Fans stepped up when, in spite of *Supernatural* winning both Favorite Sci-Fi/Fantasy Show and Favorite Network TV Drama, the cast were not invited to attend the 2012 People's Choice Awards. The Family's collective outrage was expressed to PCA, to one another and to the world at large. Their ire drew media attention and created negative buzz around the PCA. Following an article posted in *Affairs Magazine* by Charlotte Kinzie, Cookie6 responded:

> we are honoured that *Supernatural* won both awards, and furious that [...] our wins

*Figure 2: Fan art conveys how much* Supernatural *means to one fan*

were not publically acknowledged. PCA and CBS, you picked the wrong fandom to disrespect – if you think our voting is loud and passionate, wait til [*sic*] you hear our fury.

The 2013 People's Choice Awards very publicly included stars Ackles and Padalecki as presenters when *Supernatural* again won Favorite Sci-Fi Show. It is somewhat ironic that the *SPN* Family also won the new Favorite TV Fan Following category.

### The family fandom built

The *Supernatural* Family dynamic bleeds into the way fans identify with the world. Fans proclaim their loyalty to the show like they are taking holy vows, and *Supernatural* becomes embedded in the stories they tell about their lives, their language and their behaviours. As one fan shares:

> SUPERNATURAL. Idk what this word means to you, but for me, it means A LOT. It means love, it means fun, it means one hundred tears I've shared because of the boys. Yeah, the Winchesters. Supernatural is more than just a series for me, it's one of my biggest loves and I can't freaking deny it. For me, Supernatural will never really end. It will continue with me. Forever. BTW, thanks you, Eric Kripke. (Supernatural Family Fandom Fanatics, 2012)

For these fans, the *SPN* Family has become a larger-than-life entity in and of itself. Stories shared by individual members reflect Family stories and history and serve to reify Family identity. Becoming part of the *SPN* Family brings fans into a larger world where they are accepted, supported and can fight the good fight and protect their own. They are empowered by their membership and what it represents. No matter the issue, the cause, or the project, the *SPN* Family has their backs. Perhaps this is best summarized by adinari, who posted an image of Sam and Dean leaning against the Impala on a road overlooking mountains and trees, and surrounded by a blue, blue sky. The text reads: 'The show may not be perfect. The fandom may be crazy. But all it takes is hearing 'Carry On My Wayward Son' to remind me how much it means to me. I love this show so damn much.' ●

**Family Don't End With Blood: Building the *Supernatural* Family**
Mary Frances Casper

~~~~~~~~~~~

**GO FURTHER**

**Books**

*Jealous Gods and chosen people: The mythology of the Middle East*
David Leeming
(New York: Oxford University Press, 2004)

*TV living: Television, culture and everyday life*
David Gauntlett and Annette Hill
(London: Routledge, 1999)

*Other people's myths*
Wendy Doniger O'Flaherty
(New York: Macmillan Publishing Company, 1988)

*The Interpretation of Cultures: Selected Essays*
Clifford Geertz
(New York: Basic Books, 1973)

*Mythologies*
Roland Barthes
(New York: Hill and Wang, 1972)

*Myth and Reality*
Mircea Eliade
(New York: Harper & Row, Inc., 1963)

**Extracts/Essays/Articles**

'What are little gouls made of? The *Supernatural* family, fandom, and the problem of Adam'
Kristen Noone
In *Transformative Works and Cultures*. 4 (2010) [Online], http://journal.
transformativeworks.org/index.php/twc/article/view/136/159.

'American dreaming and cultural ethnocentrism: A critical discorse analysis of the mythic discourse in the US State Department's Shared Values Initiative' [Doctoral dissertation]
Mary Frances Casper

(North Dakota State University, 2007)

'Theorizing cultural identifications'
Mary Jane Collier
In W. B. Gudykunst (ed.). *Theorizing about Intercultural Communication* (Thousand Oaks, CA: Sage, 2005 pp.235-256).

'Narrativity, myth, and metaphor: Louise Erdrich and Raymond Carver talk about love'
M. J. Downes
In *MELUS*. 21:2 (1996), pp. 49–61.

**Film/Television**

'Lucifer Rising', Eric Kripke dir. *Supernatural* (Los Angeles: Warner Brothers, 2008)

'Mystery Spot', Kim Manners dir. *Supernatural* (Los Angeles: Warner Brothers, 2008)

'No Rest For the Wicked', Kim Manners dir. *Supernatural*
(Los Angeles: Warner Brothers, 2008)

'Wendigo', David Nutter dir. *Supernatural* (Los Angeles: Warner Brothers, 2005)

*Supernatural*, Eric Kripke, creator (Warner Brothers, Los Angeles 2005–)

**Online**

'Supernatural Family Fandom Fanatics' [Facebook group], https://www.facebook.com/pages/Supernatural-Family-Fandom-Fanatics/181266895303851.

*Winchester Bros*, http://www.winchesterbros.com/

*The Winchester Family Business*, http://www.thewinchesterfamilybusiness.com/

'Follow your Supernatural family'
Colleen Bement
*Examiner*. 23 January 2012, http://www.examiner.com/article/follow-your-supernatural-family.

'*Supernatural* fans call for an apology from People's Choice Awards'
Charlotte Kinzie

Family Don't End With Blood: Building the *Supernatural* Family
Mary Frances Casper

*Affairs Magazine*. 13 January 2012, http://affairsmagazine.com/
wordpress2/2012/01/13/supernatural-fans-call-for-apology-from-peoples-choice-
awards/

'*Supernatural*': Jared Padalecki talks horseback riding and his charitable causes
Mackenzie
Carina A. Mackenzie
*Zap2it.com*. 14 March 2011, http://blog.zap2it.com/frominsidethebox/2011/03/
supernatural-jared-padalecki-talks-horseback-riding-and-his-charitable-causes.html.

mrs_jarpad [Twitter],
https://twitter.com/Mrs_Jarpad.

adinari,, 2012a. *Supernatural Family* [Tumblr].
http://www.tumblr.com/tagged/supernatural-family

adinari,, 2012b. *Supernatural Family* [Tumblr]
http://25.media.tumblr.com/tumblr_lrtrj0Wl5e1r0v5upo1_400.jpg

allthechickflickmoments, 2012. *Supernatural Family* [Tumblr]
http://www.tumblr.com/tagged/supernatural-family

ccaastiel, 2012. *Supernatural Family* [Tumblr]
http://www.tumblr.com/tagged/supernatural-family

davidsdoublebanana, 2012. *Supernatural Family* [Tumblr]
http://www.tumblr.com/tagged/supernatural-family

hunterinabrowncoat, 2012. *Supernatural Family* [Tumblr]
http://www.tumblr.com/tagged/supernatural-family

invisiblecakes, 2012. *Supernatural Family* [Tumblr]
http://www.tumblr.com/tagged/supernatural-family

notrobinanymore, 2012. *Supernatural Family* [Tumblr]
http://www.tumblr.com/tagged/supernatural-family

rosettaslair, 2012. *Supernatural Family* [Tumblr]
http://www.tumblr.com/tagged/supernatural-family

scriingankhsandstars, 2012. *Supernatural Family* [Tumblr]
http://www.tumblr.com/tagged/supernatural-family

sololilia, 2012. *Supernatural Family* [Tumblr]
http://www.tumblr.com/tagged/supernatural-family

vannadear, 2012. *Supernatural Family* [Tumblr]
http://www.tumblr.com/tagged/supernatural-family

cookie6, 2012. [Online comment] People's Choice Awards. 2013 Nominees: Favorite TV
Fan Following, *Supernatural*, SPNFamily.
http://www.peopleschoice.com/pca/awards/nominees/

'People's Choice Awards: 2013 Nominees: Favorite TV Fan Following: *SPN*Family,
*Supernatural*'. *People's Choice*, http://www.peopleschoice.com/pca/awards/
nominees/

'The *Supernatural* Phenomenon – A Peek Into The Fandom'
Jennifer Pitt
*Affairs Magazine*. 11 February 2012, http://affairsmagazine.com/word-
press2/2012/02/11/the-supernatural-phenomenon-a-peek-into-the-fandom/

Chapter
6

# *Supernatural:*
# Making a Difference
# is the Meaning of Life

## Mary F. Dominiak ('Bardicvoice')

→ From the beginning of the series, with Dean's description of the Winchesters' mission as 'Saving people, hunting things – the family business' ('Wendigo' Season 1, Episode 2), *Supernatural* has advocated social activism and personal investment in helping others. Following the example set by fictional characters Sam and Dean, fans of the show adopted the first part of the Winchester family motto as their inspiration for organizing and participating in multiple charitable projects around the world, and cast and crew members further mobilized fan commitment to charity through the use of social media.

*Figure 1: The family business, 'Wendigo'*

*Supernatural* exemplifies the social mission focus that has become a hallmark of programming, particularly in the fantasy and science fiction genre, in which characters are expected not simply to save the day, but to save the world, and fans strive to follow in their footsteps.

At the heart of *Supernatural* and the heroism displayed by its characters is a basic principle that a person's awareness of the existence of evil, injustice and misfortune carries with it a personal responsibility for taking action to prevent that harm and promote good in its place. Dean stated this basic case for hunter responsibility bluntly in 'What Is and What Should Never Be' (Season 2, Episode 20): 'There are things out there in the dark. There are bad things. There are nightmare things. And people have to be saved and if we don't save them, then nobody will.' In the show's canon, Sam and Dean were initially raised by their father to hunt both for their own protection and to avenge the death of their mother, while saving anyone else they could along the way. Despite occasional doubts through the years, they have continued to hunt, but episodes in every season have established that a large part of their sense of obligation has always come from knowing they have key knowledge and skills most other people lack. The brothers recognize that ordinary people stand little chance against the overwhelming odds posed by supernatural threats precisely because they aren't equipped either to recognize the danger or to take steps to defend against it. Because Sam and Dean, as hunters,

## *Supernatural:* Making a Difference is the Meaning of Life
Mary F. Dominiak ('Bardicvoice')

*Figure 2: The alternate universe of 'What Is And What Should Never Be'*

*Figure 3: Sarah from 'Provenance'*

have the knowledge and the ability, they feel a duty to help.

Other characters introduced to the hunters' world have often cooperated actively with the brothers for the same reason, accepting as a duty the need to help and protect others for whom they feel responsible. One typical example of such a non-hunter was Sarah from 'Provenance' (Season 1, Episode 19):

Look, you guys are probably crazy, but if you're right about this? Then me and my Dad sold this painting that got these people killed. Look I'm not saying I'm not scared because I am scared as hell but … I'm not going to run and hide either.

Most such characters made only single appearances, but others, such as Lisa Braeden and Sheriff Jody Mills, became integral parts of the brothers' extended family whether or not they became hunters in any sense themselves. They went out of their way to provide help and a sense of belonging, and that made them co-heroes with the brothers.

The show also explicitly recognized early on that helping others has the benefit of making the helper feel better. That principle was laid out in 'Wendigo' during the same speech that delineated the 'family business'. Answering Sam's question about how Dean and their father could deal with the burden, Dean nodded at the civilians they were trying to protect and said: 'Well for one, them. I mean, I figure our family's so screwed

*Figure 4: Dean and Lisa, 'Exile on Main Street' (Season 6, Episode 1)*

*Figure 5: Sheriff Jody Mills, 'Slash Fiction' (Season 7, Episode 6)*

to hell, maybe we can help some others. Makes things a little bit more bearable.' Despite later questioning the price they paid for hunting, particularly in terms of the normal dreams they'd given up and the deaths of nearly everyone close to them, they kept going. The sense that their ability to help and even save people made all the loss and effort worthwhile resurfaced to bolster them in such episodes as 'What Is and What Should Never Be', 'Monster Movie' (Season 4, Episode 5) and 'The Real Ghostbusters' (Season 5, Episode 9).

Finally, through the relationship of the Winchester brothers themselves and their interactions with others, the show has always promoted the virtue of caring for others as family, whether that family was born of blood or – as personified by the characters of venerable hunter Bobby Singer and troubled angel Castiel – developed through association. From the very beginning of the series, the Winchester brothers assigned an extraordinary value, born of longing for the unattainable, to the everyday things most people take for granted. They advocated other people doing ordinary things, living the ordinary lives they, as hunters, believed they couldn't have. The brothers always enjoined people – even some already in the hunter community, like Jo in 'No Exit' (Season 2, Episode 6) and Lee and his daughter Krissy in 'Adventures In Babysitting' (Season 7, Episode 11) – not to go looking for supernatural trouble, but to concentrate instead on fulfilling their obligations to the people around them.

The show's on-screen poster boys for internalizing and expanding on these key messages of taking responsibility for others and valuing the sense of making a positive difference in the world were the characters Demian and Barnes from 'The Real Ghostbusters', which aired in November 2009. They represented the television fan community in the guise of fans of the fictional book series about Sam and Dean established in the episode 'The Monster at the End of This Book' (Season 4, Episode 18). Presented with a real supernatural emergency, the fanboys rose to the occasion and saved the day despite their own fear precisely because that's what their fictional heroes would have done. Later in the same episode, explaining why they were fans, Demian observed:

All right. In real life, he sells stereo equipment. I fix copiers. Our lives suck. But to be

### *Supernatural:* **Making a Difference is the Meaning of Life**
Mary F. Dominiak ('Bardicvoice')

*Figure 6: Demian and Barnes cosplay Sam and Dean in 'The Real Ghostbusters'*

Sam and Dean, to wake up every morning and save the world, to have a brother who would die for you – well, who wouldn't want that?

'Through their fandom activities, the characters sought to share vicariously in the greater purpose apparent in the lives of the fictional Sam and Dean.

Long before Demian and Barnes were created to mirror the real-life fandom, the show's message of being responsible for and taking action to help others resonated with fans. In place of the Winchester brothers fighting the show's supernatural evil and imaginary monsters, fans grouped together to take on real-world problems ranging from animal rescue to cancer research, community improvement projects, literacy education, suicide prevention and humanitarian aid for the homeless and for victims of natural disasters. Collective fan efforts often adapted the Winchester family business motto to suit their charitable mission statements. For example, Fandom Rocks, a fan-run charity that operated from June 2007 until June 2010, used as its slogan, 'Helping people, changing things: the fandom business.' Support Supernatural, an effort begun in 2008 and still ongoing, promotes the show while aiding A Dog's Life Rescue, the preferred charity of series star Jared Padalecki, and terms its mission 'raising awareness while raising funds'. Following the death from lung cancer of *Supernatural* director and executive producer Kim Manners in January 2009, fans on LiveJournal, such as pocket-fulof, immediately organized donations in his memory to the American Cancer Society, and individual fans have continued to support cancer research both in his name and in the name of Cecily Adams, the late wife of *Supernatural* actor Jim Beaver. Fan-run conventions such as 'Kazcon' (2007–09) and 'WinchesterCon' (founded as a *Supernatural* fandom event in 2007, and expanded to a panfandom event under the name 'Wincon' in 2010) have included charity auctions as a regular convention feature, benefiting such varied causes as homeless shelters, cancer research and loans to women creating businesses in developing countries. Fan-run show websites *Winchester Bros.com* and *The Winchester Family Business.com*, among others, have organized charity auctions.

Responding to the initiative for good displayed spontaneously by fans, the *Supernatural* cast and crew began to use their connections with fans, particularly through Twitter, Facebook, website postings and convention appearances, to mobilize fan support for charitable causes. For example, every year following Kim Manners' death, First Assistant Director Kevin Parks has garnered fan sponsorship through the Internet for his 'Team Supernatural' participation in the BC Ride to Conquer Cancer. In January 2010, following the earthquake that devastated Haiti, actor Misha Collins created a do-

Figure 7: Web logos from
Supernatural-related charity
campaigns

nation page on the UNICEF website for his Twitter followers in 2010 – affectionately called 'Misha's Minions' – to contribute to Haiti relief. Impressed by the immediate and generous response of the fans, Collins subsequently set up his own non-profit organization, Random Acts, which has continued the charitable mission to Haiti while also encouraging a host of additional independent acts of charity or just simple kindness. In late 2011, when Jared Padalecki and his wife Genevieve announced they were expecting a child, they suggested donations to St Jude Children's Hospital instead of gifts to the family, and the total collected by the resulting drive organized by the fan administrators of *Winchester Bros* was matched by the Padaleckis, as noted on *Supernatural* Wiki. Fans turned out in 2012 to support Jensen Ackles's family's efforts on behalf of the Down Syndrome Guild of Dallas – Team Levi.

*Supernatural* is not unique in the phenomenon of its fans rallying to charitable social causes. The entertainment world has a long history of social activism, with musicians and sports figures as well as actors using their fame and fan followings to attract attention and donations to worthy causes. The Live Aid concert in 1985 collected for the famine in Ethiopia. Farm Aid in 1985 and successive years supported local agriculture in the United States. The 9/11 Concert for New York City in 2001 and the Superstorm Sandy Relief Concert in 2012 responded to major tragedies and disasters. Actors have frequently encouraged their fans to support causes of importance to them: examples include George Clooney, Harrison Ford, Zachary Levi, Robert Redford and Ian Somerhalder, as noted by *Look to the Stars.com*.

Charitable activity by fans can have several underlying motives. Fandom by its very nature tends toward the creation of communities because a fandom consists of people who share at least one compelling interest, whether it's a show, book, film, sport, team, musical group or something else. People coming together and enjoying that common interest usually want the experience to continue. In the cut-throat world of television ratings and competition, fans often seek ways to promote their shows in the hope of growing their audience and convincing networks they should be renewed. Achievements in charitable work can qualify as news for reporting outlets that handle public interest stories, and the positive connection of a show and its fans to a 'good news' story of general interest can generate good publicity for the show. Accordingly, numerous shows have seen the formation of fan groups that rallied to support charities in the name of their shows both for the sake of the charity and to draw positive media attention to the show. Recent examples particularly facilitated by the expan-

*Supernatural:* **Making a Difference is the Meaning of Life**
Mary F. Dominiak ('Bardicvoice')

sion of communication afforded by the Internet include *Roswell* (Jonathon Dukes, WB, 1999-2002) (RoswellOracle); all the shows created by Joss Whedon, including *Buffy The Vampire Slayer* (WB, 1997-2003), *Angel* (WB, 1999-2004) and particularly *Firefly* (Fox, 2002-2003)/*Serenity*(2005) (Can't Stop the Serenity); and *Battlestar Galactica* (Glen A. Larson, Sci-Fi Channel, 2003-2009) (Checkers Green). As noted earlier, this is also the stated mission of Support Supernatural.

Fans also have an understandable personal interest in the charitable works of the actors and other celebrities they follow. Supporting the celebrity's causes can be a way of connecting or sharing experience and interests with the celebrity, whether or not that sharing is recognized. Organizing or participating in charitable works has some-times allowed a fan to connect with and be recognized by a celebrity, but far more fans contribute to a charitable total than are ever seen by or identified by name to their idol. The desire for recognition may play a role, but it's apparently not the principal one for most fans.

While fans have organized charity campaigns to attract attention and publicity to a show, much fandom-driven charity has also been done with no formal connection to any celebrity or specific show, and even with attempts to avoid publicity outside the fan community. One example was the fan-run charity auction known as Sweet Charity conducted on the LiveJournal blog platform. Between 2006 and 2010, fans in multiple, predominantly genre, fandoms, including *Supernatural*, offered their creative services for sale twice a year to other fans, whether to write fanfiction stories, create graphics, edit music videos, sew or even bake, with all the proceeds going to charity (see Fanlore Wiki). Because many participants were concerned that publicity might draw allegations of copyright violation from networks, studios and publishers, especially since money was being exchanged for fan-created transformative works based on television shows, books and movies, the organizers of Sweet Charity deliberately tried to limit publicity about the auctions to fannish venues, even requesting the auction not be mentioned by name in the 2010 newsletter of its primary charity recipient, RAINN (Rape, Abuse, and Incest National Network), when RAINN wanted to recognize Sweet Charity as its big-gest fund-raiser, as noted by sweetcharityvox. For the participants, contributing to the success of the auction, whether by selling their skills or buying fanworks created by oth-ers, was its own reward. After Sweet Charity closed, its code platform was used by the LiveJournal community help_haiti in 2011 to organize and run fan auctions supporting post-earthquake restoration in Haiti.

As noted, many factors beyond pure altruism may contribute to fan decisions con-cerning charitable activity. These may include seeking to use publicity to support a show; feeling connected with a celebrity by contributing to a cause they endorse; and possibly being recognized by a celebrity because of their charitable work. But while those factors may help shape the specific form a fan's charitable expression takes, in-cluding which specific charities they choose to support, they don't explain the basic impulse to be charitable. And they don't explain the passion and prevalence of charitable expression particularly in the fandom community, or the consistency of fan participation in ongoing charitable efforts over a period of years, not simply in immediate response to disasters.

This is where the social message at the heart of genre programming in general and *Supernatural* in particular appears to come into play. While characters in such mainstream television dramas as doctor, lawyer, firefighter and police/investigator shows routinely do solve problems and help people, their focus tends to be on the immediate problem, the specific case. Genre programs such as *Supernatural, Buffy, Firefly, Star Trek* (Gene Roddenberry, CBS, 1966-1968) *Battlestar Galactica* and *Revolution* (Eric Kripke, NBC, 2012 - ), on the other hand, often tend to paint their individual stories against a broader canvas of social obligation to a greater cause, whether that cause is saving the world, fighting for ethical principles, or trying to preserve or restore a society. By its nature, then, this type of genre programming encourages social activism precisely because that concept is integral to the show, its stories and its characters, and is part of the message fans take away from watching it.

In *Supernatural*, the heroes of the show, the characters with whom fans empathize and identify, feel direct personal responsibility for the safety and well-being of others; they consider it their duty to help others to the extent they can, to save strangers, even at great personal cost to themselves. Once they've recognized a problem or danger, they don't consider it enough to wait for someone else to act; they accept personal responsibility for taking action themselves, believing if they didn't act, the consequences of inaction would be on them. They stand for the idea that making a difference – doing something, however great or small, to help others and make the world a better, safer place – is what gives meaning to life. They haven't been able to save everyone they set out to help, but that hasn't stopped them from trying, and in the show, their selflessness and sacrifice have saved the world.

That's an amazingly powerful message, and one designed to inspire fans to real-world heroism of their own – like their heroes, not in expectation of reward or recognition, but because it's the right thing to do. Because they are responsible for other people, and it's the way they, too, can save others. For the fans of *Supernatural*, awareness of problems such as disease, homelessness, disaster losses and abuse has become analogous to hunters recognizing the plagues of demons, ghosts and monsters. Banding together with each other to support organizations equipped to help the human and animal victims of those problems is a way fans, like hunters, can effectively fight back to save as many as they can.

Quite apart from activities intentionally promoting the show or responding to major disasters, the impulse to communal charity has become the *Supernatural* fans' spontaneous response to almost any milestone involving the show or its cast and crew. For example, the desire by fans to celebrate the announcements of the impending births of

**Supernatural: Making a Difference is the Meaning of Life**
Mary F. Dominiak ('Bardicvoice')

children to cast members Collins and Padalecki resulted immediately in the organization of drives for donations to the actors' preferred child-related charities. Among fans of the show, giving to others has become a routine way of sharing joy and expressing solidarity by collectively doing something positive. Sharing this experience of helping others further helps to cement a sense of being part of a community, a member of a family, and bolsters relationships among the individual fans who have joined in a common cause.

*Supernatural* has proven to be much more than a simple horror show on television, and its underlying messages of personal and social responsibility and community have produced real-world effects. Saving people and making a difference for the better has become the *Supernatural* fandom business, the collective job of the fandom family. That's something Sam and Dean Winchester would approve. ●

## GO FURTHER

### Film/Television

'Wendigo'  David Nutter, dir. *Supernatural* (Los Angeles: Warner Brothers,  2005)
'What Is and What Should Never Be', Eric Kripke, dir. *Supernatural* (Los Angeles: Warner
  Brothers 2007)

'Provenance', David Ehrman, dir. *Supernatural* (Los Angeles: Warner Brothers, 2006)
'Exile on Main Street', Phil Sgriccia, dir. *Supernatural* (Los Angeles: Warner Brothers,
  2010)

'Slash Fiction", John Showalter, dir. *Supernatural* (Los Angeles: Warner Brothers, 2011)
'The Real Ghostbusters' James L. Conway, dir. *Supernatural* (Los Angeles: Warner
  Brothers, 2009).

'No Exit', Kim Manners, dir. *Supernatural* (Los Angeles: Warner Brothers, 2006)
'Adventures In Babysitting', Jeannot Szwarc,  dir. *Supernatural* (Los Angeles: Warner
  Brothers,  2012)

'The Monster at the End of This Book', Mike Rohl, dir. *Supernatural* (Los Angeles:
  Warner Brothers, 2006)

### Online

'The history of Can't Stop the Serenity.' *Can't Stop the Serenity (CSTS)* [Wordpress],
  2011, http://www.cantstoptheserenity.com/about/history-2/.
'On The Flight Deck: BSG Cast Charity Projects.' *Checkers Green*, 8 February 2012,
  http://www.checkersgreen.com/.

'Misha's Minions'
Misha Collins
*UNICEF*. 13 January 2010, http://inside.unicefusa.org/site/
TR?pxfid=13831&bpg=rlist&post_id=3940&type=fr_tribute_fund&fr_
id=1090&pg=fund&lcmd=top&lcmd_cf=.

'Campaign Five: Final Donations and Closing Our Doors.'
Dana
*Fandom Rocks*. 15 June 2010, http://www.fandom-rocks.com/.

*Supernatural*: Making a Difference is the Meaning of Life
Mary F. Dominiak ('Bardicvoice')

'Sweet Charity', *Fanlore* Wiki. 12 May 2012, http://fanlore.org/wiki/Sweet_Charity.

'Relevant to Your Interests'
help_haiti (pseud.)
*LiveJournal*. 12 January 2011, http://help-haiti.livejournal.com/

'Kazcon: A Supernatural Convention'
kazcon (pseud.)
*LiveJournal*. 24 September 2009, http://kazcon.livejournal.com/

'George Clooney Charity Works, Events and Causes.' *Look to the Stars*, 2013,
http://www.looktothestars.org/celebrity/george-clooney.

'Harrison Ford Charity Works, Events and Causes.' *Look to the Stars*, 2013,
http://www.looktothestars.org/celebrity/harrison-ford.

'Zachary Levi Charity Works, Events and Causes.' *Look to the Stars*, 2013,
http://www.looktothestars.org/celebrity/zachary-levi.

'Robert Redford Charity Works, Events and Causes.' *Look to the Stars*, 2013,
http://www.looktothestars.org/celebrity/robert-redford.

'Ian Somerhalder Charity Works, Events and Causes.' *Look to the Stars*, 2013,
http://www.looktothestars.org/celebrity/ian-somerhalder.

'The 2012 Enbridge Ride to Conquer Cancer benefiting BC Cancer Foundation –
Team Supernatural'
Kevin Parks
*BC Cancer Foundation*. 2012, http://www.conquercancer.ca/site/TR/Events/
Vancouver2012?pg=team&fr_id=1413&team_id=51461.

'donation made'
pocketfullof (pseud.)
*LiveJournal*. 4 February 2009, http://pocketfullof.livejournal.com/293039.html.

*Random Acts*, http://www.therandomact.org/

'Fan Charities.' *RoswellOracle*, 2012, http://www.roswelloracle.com/charaties.html.

'Jared thanks fandom for their charity.' *Supernatural* Wiki [Storify], 26 March 2012, http://storify.com/superwiki/jared-thanks-fandom-for-their-charity.

*Support Supernatural*, http://www.supportsupernatural.com/

'Update'
sweetcharityvox (pseud.)
*LiveJournal*. 26 May 2010, http://sweetcharityvox.livejournal.com/

'2012 Down Syndrome Guild of Dallas Buddy Walk®.' *Team Levi*, 2012, https://bos.
etapestry.com/fundraiser/DownSyndromeGuildofDallas/2012BuddyWalk/individual.
do;jsessionid=5B12DC9FB1E96755E6220A54657888F6?participationRef=607.0.55405
6493&diverted=true.

'The Winchester Family Business First Ever Charity Auction' [WFB Fandom Page]. *The
Winchester Family Business*, 2012, http://www.thewinchesterfamilybusiness.com/wfb-
fandom-page.html.

'Results of website search on "charity."' *Winchester Bros*, 9 January 2013, http://www.
winchesterbros.com/site/index.php/component/search/?searchword=charity&orderi
ng=newest&searchphrase=all.

'What is Wincon? What charity does your raffle support?' [FAQ]. *Wincon*, 2011, http://
omgwincon.com/faq/

Chapter
7

# Life Changing: *Supernatural* and the Power of Fandom

Misha Collins

→ When Lynn and Kathy first asked me to contribute a chapter to this book, I said, "No way! Leave me alone!" and threatened to take out a restraining order against them. But when I learned that they were willing to pay me more money than most people make in a lifetime to jot down a couple of pages, I said, "yes!" and then qualified that with, "but it isn't about the money, I'm writing from the heart for the love of the fans." I also asked Lynn and Kathy to flash me Mardi Gras-style--which, happily, they did.

Figure 1: Misha Collins as Castiel, 'Lazarus Rising,' (Season 4, Episode 1)

Figure 2: Misha Collins (Photo credit Christopher Schmelke)

Now, before I start, a disclaimer: This isn't an essay. It's just a ruminating ramble about how coming into contact with fandom has affected me and about how I see the community from my vantage point. My apologies in advance for the three minutes you are about to waste.

Fandom and its many fascinating aspects have, for the most part, blindsided me. Not only did I not see it coming, but previously, I was only peripherally aware of its existence. For me, discovering this fandom was pretty much like getting kidnapped by a dragon. I didn't expect being inducted into this world to be anywhere near as strange, wonderful or overwhelming as it has been. I didn't expect any of it. I remember watching the season premiere of *Supernatural* Season 4--the episode in which my character, Castiel, was introduced--with the producers and writers at a little screening party at producer McG's offices in West Hollywood. Sera Gamble, a writer and producer on the show, was standing next to me as we watched. When my character came onscreen, she leaned over and whispered to me, "Your life is about to change." I thought, "that is a truly arrogant thing for a producer of a CW television show to say. I've been on plenty of television shows. My life is going to stay exactly the same, I don't know what you're talking about." Well, Sera, I think I owe you an apology for that thought.

When I stepped into this fandom, I suppose I also, unwittingly, stepped into a "celebrity" role (I hate nothing more than applying this term to myself.) Discovering what this role would be for me has been an interesting process. The first thing I noticed was that there are myriad expectations as to how a "celebrity" (yes I'm still employing quotes) behaves and how "fans" (there you get quotes too) are supposed to behave. Without even being conscious of these normative behaviors, we intuitively follow them. We know how somebody who is a "celebrity" is supposed to dress, smile and interact with their fans (okay, I'm giving up on the quotes). I don't want to fall into that expected dynamic; however, I notice that when I stop paying attention, I automatically do. It's interesting to see how readily behaving normally becomes the easiest choice. There's a certain set of basic rules that actors coming into celebrity almost inherently understand and unthinkingly adopt. You know that you're supposed to interact with your fans in a certain distant, reserved, almost regal manner, and so you do. People simultaneously want you to be just like them, and somehow special. And so you play the role of the regular guy who's secretly awesome. Why do we play into these dynamics? Who wrote the script? Celebrity space is such a peculiar and specific space that you would think not everyone would know those rules, but we all do. It's frankly amazing. We have all absorbed these cultural norms for behavior, and there's an interesting kind of discomfort when you don't do what you're "supposed to do" in a given situation.

I don't know how to make sense of it; in fact, I think maybe trying to make sense of it is a futile endeavor. I'm largely in a position where fantasies are projected onto me: People like to imagine that I'm like the character I play on TV, or that I'm secretly screw-

**Life Changing: *Supernatural* and the Power of Fandom**
Misha Collins

*Figure 3: Collins at a fan convention (photo credit Karen Cooke)*

*Figure 4: Collins chats with fans (photo credit Karen Cooke)*

ing Jensen in my trailer, or that I am somehow a perfect man or that I'm an unselfconscious maverick. And while I am, in fact, perfect, not all of the other stuff is true. So I've stepped into this role where people are projecting fantasy onto me. Fans do it to Jared and Jensen and dozens of other TV actors as well. And while I think it's all quite arbitrary and silly, there's a part of me, my ego, who loves the attention and can't help thinking: "Shit, I am pretty cool." So there's this dynamic where I am well aware of the fact that these are undeserved affections, but at the same time, I grin and say: "Okay, bring it on,

I'll take the job." And it's very difficult to take that job and not let your ego sweep you away. It must be strange for anybody who's in a similar position. You get showered with this adoration and praise and you just have to learn to graciously say, "thank you" and keep working.

When I went to my first fan convention in New Jersey, in my first few minutes on-stage I realized I just couldn't do what everyone expected. I tried to answer the questions, but I just felt like, a) this is too boring; and b) I don't know enough about the show to answer the questions accurately. The average fan knows a lot more about it than I do! So I just started playing with it to make it more fun for me. And before I knew it, as the months went by, that became my onstage character. It's funny, the same thing happens when you're building a character for a show. You just start playing with stuff, and then certain things become codified and that's how that character remains. I think that's what happened with Castiel on *Supernatural*, with his physicality, vocal quality, and the way he stares blankly at people. None of that was based on conscious decisions, but little things that fell into place, and then that just became how it was. That's part of what happened with me onstage and with Twitter as well. Although on Twitter, I was more consciously satirizing the self-important celebrity from the beginning.

At some point, fairly early into this strange experiment, I realized that my position on the show would allow me to provide a framework within which people can engage one another in the community. That I could be a catalyst because I happened to have been cast on a show that people were really, really enthused about. And so I guess I partly saw it as my responsibility to be a coalescing factor. Or perhaps a better way to put that is I saw it as an opportunity to serve and to help others be of service. So now I can say "Let's all go do a scavenger hunt" or "Let's go help Haiti" and people will come along and participate and engage.

It became apparent fairly quickly that there was tremendous creative potential in *Supernatural* fandom. In spite of what everyone seems to think, I don't spend a lot of time trolling online, but people email me things or I occasionally click through on something in the Twitter feed, and I see a tremendous amount of creative energy. Fan conventions are rife with spectacular fan art. It was astonishing to me how talented and hard-working people were. It is stunning how much money, time and creative energy go into being a fan. I started Random Acts with the ambition of harnessing those resources to playful, productive and compassionate ends. One of my objectives was to make RA crowd-sourced, instead of about what I, Misha, am doing. I was just trying to find a way to facilitate fans doing charitable work together – and it's largely working. This past year we raised nearly $500,000 and have completed projects far beyond the scope of what I ever imagined possible. It's something that makes me both grateful and proud.

Fans are generally nerds. They're people who are more thoughtful than your average person and also a little more devoted. They're people who can obsess over things, and really get into the minutiae, and who may also be more likely to step into a fantasy world.

## Life Changing: *Supernatural* and the Power of Fandom
Misha Collins

*Figure 5: Fans volunteer with Random Acts to build an orphanage in Haiti*

They spend more time at their computers, more time reading books, more time imagining. I think genre and fantasy shows like *Supernatural* appeal to these people, and I think that disproportionately, those are also people who are seeking greater community in their lives. I've met a lot of people in fandom who for one reason or another have felt like they don't totally fit in to normal society. For them, this fandom has served as a conduit to finding one another—it has helped them forge community. And I think, in a nutshell, that feeling of community is what makes fandom so powerful.

I did a global scavenger hunt for the past two years called GISHWHES (the Greatest International Scavenger Hunt the World Has Ever Seen). At every convention since, at least a half-dozen people have come up to me and said something, sometimes (no joke) with tears welling in their eyes, about how transformative the experience was for them. Their best friends are now people they met on their team, or their roommates are people they met on their team, or they were agoraphobic and hadn't left the house for years and now a curtain has been lifted. I met a woman who had not been out of her house in three years before participating in GISHWHES. She was trembling and crying; it had been a major breakthrough for her. When I hear things like that, I can't help tearing up myself. It makes this job that I have lucked into so much more fulfilling. For some people, fandom is an essential and powerful force in their lives. For others, fandom serves as a whimsical little romp or an erotic fantasy or a writing workshop. For me, Sera Gamble was right – fandom has changed my life. ●

*Figure 6: The house that Random Acts built*

## GO FURTHER

### Film/Television

'Lazarus Rising,' Kim Manners, dir. *Supernatural* (Los Angeles: Warner Brothers, 2008)

# 'I'M THE ONE WHO GRIPPED YOU TIGHT AND RAISED YOU FROM PERDITION.'

**CASTIEL TO DEAN IN 'LAZARUS RISING'**
SEASON 4, EPISODE 1

# Fan Appreciation no.2
# Serge Ladouceur: The Cinematographer

**Interview by Sarah House and Lynn Zubernis**

Figure 1: 'All Dogs Go to
Heaven' (Season 6, Episode 8).

**Sarah House and Lynn Zubernis (SH&LZ):** *One of* Supernatural's *most recognized elements is its trademark cinematography. Dark themes are enhanced by the strikingly dark palette of colors, which obscure as often as they illuminate, mirroring Sam and Dean's journey to hell and back again, and again, and again. Working closely with the director of each episode, Director of Photography Serge Ladouceur has been the talent behind* Supernatural's *distinctive look since Season 1.*

*As a teenager, Serge already knew he wanted to become a cinematographer.*

**Serge:** I was interested in light, visual representation, photography and painting – but also in storytelling. I was attracted by the power of motion pictures as way of expression. It is said that we attract what we want to have. I guess I did attract these projects [like Supernatural] because I basically like the horror/fantasy genre. I enjoy the genre both as a spectator and as a film-maker. I like to create atmospheres for the audience. The film noir movement, which has its roots in the German expressionism, is definitely a big influence. I can also pinpoint the French New Wave (nouvelle vague), with its free form and spontaneous camera work, as an influence.

**SH&LZ:** *Serge shared his insights on making the show look fabulous, and*

**Fan Appreciation no.2**
Serge Ladouceur: The Cinematographer

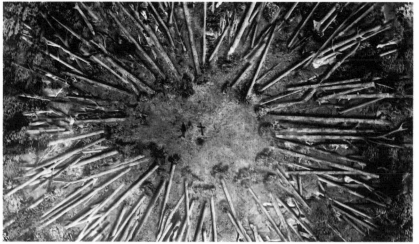

_Figure 2: 'After School_
_Special'._

_Figure 3: 'Lazarus Rising'._

answered fans' questions about some of our favourite moments.

Supernatural excels in striking images, carefully constructed to convey meaning and emotion. The architecture of the distinctive bridge in 'All Dogs Go to Heaven' (Figure 1) has been interpreted as symbolizing the constant heavy weight Sam and Dean have on their shoulders. The lines of the bridge, the fence and even the angled stream of light, draw the viewer's eye to the centre of the frame, as the giant bridge looms above the brothers and makes them look small and alone. Similarly, in 'After School Special' (Season 4, Episode 13), the building looms, setting up the element of danger and threat. The outside world is beautifully reflected in the windows, creating a sense of imprisonment enhanced by the bars on the windows and the crisscrossing concrete (Figure 2). The menace the viewer feels is later confirmed when it is revealed that the building is a psychiatric hospital. Is the process of creating meaning as intentional as fans like to think?

**Serge:** We do not necessarily ask ourselves all the time, what is the symbolism behind a particular framing or move, although we will sometimes. Most of the time our instinct tells us that this is the thing to do, that this particular element must be used. Of course, an image is never without meaning and as storytellers we're aware of its power. The meaning can be implied or obvious, but the framing and the lighting always have a purpose.

**SH&LZ:** The aftermath of Dean's resurrection (Figure 3) is an iconic shot on Supernatural. Although it's a partially computer-generated image, there are a number of elements that tie into other recurring visuals on the show, such as the shadow of the cross in the centre of the giant circle. Fans noticed the similarity of this overhead shot to the close-up of Dean's eye as the camera zooms into his Hell in 'No Rest for the Wicked' (Season 3, Episode 16). Fans have also hypothesized that the image visually references the aftermath of the famous Tunguska event, which occurred in Russia in 1908. Kim Manners, who directed this episode, also directed the episode of the X-Files (Chris Carter, Fox, 1993-2002) called 'Tunguska', in which Mulder and Krycek travel to where it happened and find the event is linked to the aliens of that series' myth arc. Serge conveyed his recollection of this shot, emphasizing the collaborative nature of the artistic decisions made on Supernatural, and the potential for multiple influences and interpretations.

**Fan Appreciation no.2**
Serge Ladouceur: The Cinematographer

*Figure 4: 'When the Levee Breaks'.*

**Serge:** I believe the first intention (and it is too bad that Kim is not here anymore to answer this question) was to simply tell this story and convey the idea that something very powerful had just happened. But we can ask ourselves: what happens subconsciously when we make an artistic decision? What mechanisms are at work when we set things in motion in order to create a shot? There are many people involved in the creation of a shot. The director is of course the first resource and has the final word, but many other creators are collaborators in the process and bring their own experience and imagery.

**SH&LZ:** *Another striking image which is valued by fans appears in the episode 'Scarecrow' Season 1, Episode 11), an overhead shot of a cluster of black umbrellas in a rainstorm. That episode was also directed by Kim Manners.*

**Serge:** There's a story about that shot. That's also a crane shot. When this was edited Kim was here and when they got it they had edited that shot out. Kim insisted that this shot must be back in. Kim always had exactly in his mind what he wanted the scene to look like. He had each shot played in his mind. His script was all written over, full of notes. And he knew exactly what he was doing. He wasn't shooting a lot of possibilities, he was shooting only what he wanted to see in the end.

*The time spent setting up a shot varies with its complexity. Sam's time in the panic room in 'When the Levee Breaks' (Season 4, Episode 12) is conveyed through a number of brilliantly shot sequences. Here the camera pulls up to reveal that Sam is hallucinating (Figure 4).*

*This striking overhead shot gives us three recurring images at once – the circle, the cross and the star. Sam is entrapped inside the circle and his body resembles that of an inverted cross, overlaid on the devil's trap. The star and sigils on the floor, to fans, have become synonymous with* Supernatural. *The overhead fan and skylight provide opportunities to create some gorgeous effects, such as the pools of circular light surrounding Sam.*

**Serge:** Working in this kind of set requires preparation. The lighting is discussed ahead of time and the rigging crew will set the main lights a few days before filming. In this particular set, a catwalk was installed on top of the set so we could access easily the lighting that was set around the small opening where there was a fan with a propeller-style blade. One thing worth noting is the execution of the move described above in regards to the lighting. Director Robert Singer told me two weeks before about his intention of doing this shot. The shot involved the use of a crane installed outside the set with the remote head reaching inside, close to Jared and pulling back to the overhead shot. Lighting was not going to be an easy task because the arm of the crane and the remote head are quite big and take a lot of room, so the potential for camera shadow or rig shadow is important. At the same time, you want to end up with a lighting that is good and uncompromised. That was a tough one.

**SH&LZ:** *Outdoor scenes shot in beautiful Vancouver are often stunning. The scene in 'Good God Y'All' (Season 5, Episode 2) where Sam and Dean struggle with the decision of whether to stay together is not only beautiful, it also emphasizes just how small our two very human heroes are. Against this huge vista, they look almost fragile (Figure 5). This is the scene where Sam decides to leave Dean, so it works perfectly to create a sense of the brothers' impending loneliness.*

*What lighting, perspective and distance decisions were used to convey the emotional impact of this scene?*

**Serge:** The backlight is instrumental to the mood here. While outside, I will favour the use of backlight or side light as opposed to front light. Also

**Fan Appreciation no.2**
Serge Ladouceur: The Cinematographer

_____

*Figure 5: 'Good God, Y'All'.*

_____

*Figure 6: 'Clap Your Hands If
You Believe'.*

Figure 7: 'Jump The Shark'.

the fact that we are not seeing any part of the sky emphasizes the heaviness of the world around them. This is a case of using a long lens for a wide shot, meaning that the camera has to be at some distance from the actors to get this composition.

**SH&LZ:** *Sam and Dean have many of their heart to hearts during the 'Impala scenes'. Often, there is a backdrop of majestic hills, green fields or crystal blue lakes. In the ending scene of 'Clap Your Hands If You Believe' (Season 6, Episode 9), the backdrop is power poles, which seem to break up the 'perfection' of the boys' surroundings – just as Sam is 'imperfect' without his soul, refusing the tradition of sharing a beer with his brother (Figure 6). Were the power lines deliberately included?*

**Serge:** They were part of the location that was chosen and instead of fighting and avoiding them I used them as part of the composition.

**SH&LZ:** *Does a director ask the location finders to find such a place to create this shot or does it work the other way around, the location finders have a list of possible locations and a director picks one that suits his needs?*

**Serge:** It can happen both ways. The director will express his views and the location team, in concert with the art department, will present him with options. Very often the art department will have a collection of possible locations to present to the director when he arrives for the prep. The production designer is also instrumental in this regard.

**SH&LZ:** *In 'Jump The Shark' (Season 4, Episode 19), a more 'typical' backdrop of a calming sky and water creates an image of the boys living on the road (Figure 7). Sam brushing his teeth. Dean sleeping in the car. There's a feeling of momentary serenity – a time for the boys to rest before delving into their next life-threatening job. Here Serge used filters to 'paint' a beautiful picture.*

**Serge:** Technically I used a gradual neutral density filter to darken the sky and reveal the beautiful texture in the clouds. Grad NDs, as we call them, are filters that are clear on the bottom and darker towards the top with either an abrupt or smooth transition in the mid part. Different intensities are available. They are wonderful tools in the palette of the cinematographer.

**SH&LZ:** *The graveyard scene in 'Swan Song' (Season 5, Episode 22) powerfully ends a chapter in the series, beginning with this evocative shot of a rusted, worn out sign in the foreground and a road disappearing into the distance in the background (Figure 8). The gate is open, almost inviting, but there is also a tremendous sense of foreboding conveyed by the mist and dampness. The final effect, like so much on Supernatural, is a collaborative achievement.*

**Serge:** We use atmospheric smoke very often when we shoot outside, mainly at night but also during the daytime as is the case with this scene. The SFX department has different tools to produce and control the smoke.

**SH&LZ:** *The series' frequent scenes illuminated only by Sam and Dean's flashlight beams are also created with atmospheric smoke.*

**Serge:** The only way you would see a shaft of light like that is through smoke. If you don't put [in] that smoke – atmo we call it – it's the only way to show a beam of light. If you have no atmo, you can't control it. And that's another element of the show since Season 1. We've been controlling the smoke on the set to create a lighting effect or just to supplement. It's very difficult to control it.

Figure 8: 'Swan Song'.

Figure 9: 'A Little Slice of Kevin'

**Fan Appreciation no.2**
Serge Ladouceur: The Cinematographer

**SH&LZ:** *Signs are used for both humour and foreboding in* Supernatural. *In the Season 8 episode, 'A Little Slice of Kevin' (Season 8, Episode 7), a sign conveys dark humour – Kevin gets his finger cut off in this episode (Figure 9). He should have read the sign!*

**Serge:** The art department creates most of the signs. Sometimes the script calls for a specific sign and sometimes the director will ask Production Designer Jerry Wanek for a particular one. Once on the set, though, the director will decide whether he will showcase a sign or not. As the DP, I might also influence the direction of the shooting and suggest that we incorporate them in the shot. It is truly a collaborative process.

**SH&LZ:** *Season 8's flashbacks of Purgatory were striking. The desaturation of the footage, the use of lighting and the composition of the shots made the flashback scenes some of the most beautiful cinematography seen in the show (Figure 10). In stark contrast, Sam's flashback scenes in the same season were bright and colourful and almost fuzzy; in fact, they looked so surreal that many fans were certain that they were not memories, but recalled dreams or hallucinations.*

Figure 10: 'What's Up, Tiger Mommy?'

**Serge:** Director and Executive Producer Robert Singer came to me when we were shooting Jensen Ackles's episode 'Heartache' (Season 8, Episode 3) in which there was the first Sam flashback to be filmed (Jensen was shooting first but his episode was airing third) and told me he wanted to have a special look for these flashbacks. His episode was airing first but was shot after Jensen's. He said to me: 'Think of Elvira Madigan as a reference for the look.' Elvira Madigan is a Swedish film of the 1960s and has that slightly overexposed and diffuse look, and he wanted me to go in that direction. I understood what he wanted because I knew the film. I then emulated the look during the shooting. I have to say here that again this is part of a process: I shot with this concept in mind and then I transmitted the intention to the colourist in Los Angeles who refined the concept and produced the final look on the DaVinci colour correction system.

**SH&LZ:** *The overall brightness or darkness of the show has been a conscious decision, one that changed several times over the course of the series.*

**Serge:** We want *Supernatural* to look like all we witness could really happen in real life. So, for me, there is a strong reality-base bias. Lights are source justified, windows, practicals. I also work with a strong contrast ratio. The look we developed at the beginning of the first season could be technically described as follows: a bleach bypass look by which we desaturate colours and increase contrast in the timing suite. As the first season progressed, we adjusted this look and pulled back from the strong contrasty flavour of the first episodes. The so called 'informative' scenes, in which the Winchester boys research a case, were rendered with a more natural approach, meaning there was less desaturation and contrast, and the 'supernatural' scenes were rendered following our original bleach bypass concept. In the second season, we followed the recipe developed in the first season and adjusted the look according to the different stories and somehow we pulled back a little more from the original recipe in some episodes because of the comedy nature of some particular scripts. We were going to stay the course, keep it dark. But that was a wish, really more than a wish, from the network. They wanted it a little brighter. So we went along. [...] We went a little less dark and more colourful. But overall I've always felt the series is a dark series and should stay dark. I enjoyed doing that season anyway because it was an experiment. At the beginning of the fourth season, Eric Kripke told me, 'So we're staying dark.'

**Fan Appreciation no.2**
Serge Ladouceur: The Cinematographer

Figure 11: 'The Born Again
Identity'.

Figure 12: 'Hello Cruel World'

**SH&LZ:** *In 'The Born Again Identity' (Season 7, Episode 17), the use of the graffitied 'scream' (from Edvard Munch's The Scream, [1893]) in the background covered with crisscrossed lines (resembling a prison), seems to symbolize Sam's inner struggle (Figure 11). It not only foretells his future (locked in a psychiatric hospital), it also reminds us of where he has been (locked in Lucifer's cage). The rainbow colouring on the wall, the street lamp, the mist and moonlight come together to create a stunning visual.*

**Serge:** That location, host to a lot of artist studios, was wonderful because of all its graffiti. When I saw the 'scream' on the wall, I didn't want to leave it in the dark. A window nearby justified the lighting. The street lamp, provided by the art department, was put in place to complement the composition. This kind of composition happens very often on the spot.

**SH&LZ:** *Water was a recurring theme in the episode 'Hello Cruel World' (Season 7, Episode 2) (the Leviathan spread via water) and having it encroach on Sam creates a sense of danger and threat (Figure 12). The pools of light enhance this feeling as the camera pulls back for a high-angle shot to reveal that Sam is alone in this warehouse; indeed, he looks lost from this angle. The overhead lamps create circles of light, which often appear in* Supernatural, *interpreted as symbolic of the angels. Here Lucifer, the dark angel, is menacing Sam.*

**Serge:** Sometimes we say 'painting with light'; here we can also say 'painting with water'. I wanted to darken some parts of the floor so I asked the SFX department to water down some parts of the floor to create darker areas. As for the interpretation regarding the overhead lamps, they are there to also create light and dark areas in the frame. The symbolism deriving from the shot itself is subjective, as there are as many interpretations as there are viewers. My intention was to convey a sense of loneliness and coldness.

**SH&LZ:** *Castiel's appearance at the end of 'Lazurus Rising' (Season 4 Episode 1) was perhaps one of the best entrances made by any character in* Supernatural *(or ever!). The slow pan-up as the doors open, followed by the exploding lamps showering Castiel in sparks as he approaches Dean and Bobby, created a majestic and powerful entrance (Figure 13). It does, however, seem like it would be a challenge to film.*

**Serge:** I remember very well shooting this scene because it was at the

**Fan Appreciation no.2**
Serge Ladouceur: The Cinematographer

*Figure 13: 'Lazarus Rising'.*

very beginning of Season 4 and we had just transitioned from film to digital, and this was our first scene. The actual light bulbs were not exploding, in fact hundreds of sparks had been set by the FX department and the reset was very quick because they were prepared for many takes. The light bulbs were just remotely switched off as the sparks were going off around them. One of my favourite scenes too.

**SH&LZ:** *Dean's encounter with Lucifer wearing his brother's body in 'The End' (Season 5, Episode 4) is heartbreaking (Figure 14). Fans have conjectured that the statue of the woman with the water jug could represent purity, as in Greek/Roman mythology. Sam's white suit stands out as crisp and bright among the dead leaves and desaturated footage. White normally represents purity and goodness, but here it's making a mockery of that. This further emphasizes the difficulty Dean is having in wrestling with the decision about saying yes to Michael. The statue (purity) is dirty and marked, whereas evil Lucifer is bright and shiny. Things are not what they seem. The neglected garden could be symbolic of the Garden of Eden. As Adam was tempted by Eve, Dean is being tempted by Lucifer to say yes to Michael. It could also represent the Garden of Gethsemane – where Judas betrayed Jesus. Will Sam betray Dean?*

**Serge:** In the mythology of the Bible, Lucifer, before his fall, was the angel of light, the morning star, so the use of white in this case is justified by ancient myths. I think fans are getting most of the intentions here.

**SH&LZ:** *Having angel Anna land on a car with painted wings in 'The Song Remains The Same' (Season 5, Episode 13) was an inspired idea (Figure*

Figure 14: 'The End'

Figure 15: 'The Song Remains
The Same'.

**Fan Appreciation no.2**
Serge Ladouceur: The Cinematographer

*Figure 16: 'It's A Terrible Life'.*

*15). Anna is not dead at this point in the episode. Later, when she does die, we don't get the iconic 'wing shot' that we often get when an angel dies, so this may count as Anna's 'wing shot'. In order for this shot to work, the wings had to be obvious, but not too obvious.*

**Serge:** The short answer [to how we accomplished that] is wide-angle. The idea was to set the emphasis on Anna and the car while keeping everything in focus, including the people in the car. The symmetry was important to the composition because it was essential to the comprehension of the shot.

**SH&LZ:** *'It's a Terrible Life' (Season 4, Episode 17) gave the producers a chance to completely change the look of* Supernatural *– the colours, the interiors, the costumes, etc. An overhead shot captures just how out of place Sam is in this world (Figure 16). He is squashed into a cubicle, with barely enough room to fit his long legs – or even to write. The overhead shot is a great way to emphasize the sense of entrapment. The bars on the window to his right add to this effect. The bobble headed Dracula on his desk is a cheeky reminder of their actual lives. Are overhead shots more difficult? Can they be overused?*

**Serge:** Overhead shots are not more difficult than, let's say, low-angle

Figure 17: 'A Very Supernatural Christmas'.

shots where you see a large expanse of ceiling. Very low-angle shots can sometimes require more work on soundstage because most of the time the sets don't have a ceiling. We use ceiling pieces that we put in place to cover areas of ceiling seen in low-angle shots though. As for the use of overhead shots and their effect, they are part of the grammar and must be used as part of the storytelling and not systematically, because yes, they can lose their impact. They are expensive because we can't afford the crane each day – maybe an hour or two. Not having the crane all the time can be good though. It makes these shots rare.

**SH&LZ:** *Sometimes the joy fans get from a particular scene reflects the joy Serge felt in creating it. The closing shot of Sam and Dean through the window in 'A Very* Supernatural *Christmas' (Season 3, Episode 8) was so popular that it became many fans' Christmas cards (Figure 17).*

**Serge:** It took me a little while to light that scene, but I remember I had joy lighting this, because I was seeing it. We were still shooting on film at that time and on the monitor you could see the full result. I saw it in my head, and when I saw the result, I knew I did what I wanted to do – the loneliness, the sense of brotherhood, and want. Lighting provides a way to support technically what the film-maker wants so say, and the lighting is a way to express myself that's not in writing.

**SH&LZ:** *Fans spend a lot of time analysing the use of colour and what it might symbolize. Red and blue, for example seem to be significant in the show. There are a variety of interpretations on what these colours represent – often it depends on the context. One interpretation is that they*

**Fan Appreciation no.2**
Serge Ladouceur: The Cinematographer

Figure 18: 'Sympathy for the Devil'.

represent freedom – red, white and blue being the colours of the American flag. Castle Storage is significant too, because it appears in 'Bad Day at Black Rock' (John's lock-up [Season 3, Episode 3]), 'Sympathy for the Devil' (Season 5, Episode 1), and again in 'The Man Who Knew Too Much' (Season 6, Episode 22) when we see inside Sam's mind (Figure 18). The sign reflecting on the Impala adds to the beauty of the shot. Is there a colour guide for the show?

**Serge:** There is no colour guide per se but most of the time Jerry Wanek, production designer, will set a tone in prep and I will follow his lead as far as choice of colours is concerned. This is a collaborative work again, and it is done on a case-by-case basis. Some other times, I will lead the charge and implement colours I think are relevant to the mood of a particular scene. There are always two people having input for a shot. When a shot is created it is always a collaborative effort. The director expresses his intentions and the DP will translate it into an image. Another important collaborator to the creation of the imagery is the camera operator, who will also have his input. We're all collaborators, or in other words, storytellers.

**SH&LZ:** Supernatural's actors are also part of that collaboration. There are quite a few scenes in Supernatural which call for a great deal of emotion from the actors. The scene near the end of 'Heart' (Season 2, Episode 17), in which Dean reacts to the sound of his brother having to kill his lover (and unfortunately a werewolf) Madison, is one of the most powerful (Figure 19). These scenes present a different type of challenge, both for the actors and the director of photography. The end result is a collaborative effort.

Figure 19: 'Heart'.

**Serge:** Jensen has an amazing control. Some actors would put some glycerine drops in, but Jensen never does that. I don't know what state he goes through, but he can call up that space within him and he can be there and you believe it. It's amazing. But he needs the help of the people around him. There's one scene at the end of an episode where he confesses to his brother that he's been torturing [souls] in hell. When we start any scene, we usually start with the wide shot because all the elements are there, and then go tighter and tighter and you end up with the close-up. But in that scene, Jensen asked us to start with the close-up and take our way back. So we went right for the close-ups and then made our way back.

**SH&LZ:** *Sometimes it's not so much a 'what' that Serge is lighting, but*

Figure 20: 'Bloodlust'.

**Fan Appreciation no.2**
Serge Ladouceur: The Cinematographer

*a 'who'. The iconic image of Dean leaning on the Impala in 'Bloodlust'
(Season 2, Episode 3) as the sun catches his face is one of the most well-
known shots of the series (Figure 20). Was that lighting intentional?*

**Serge:** That's what we call a flare, a source of light that hits the lens and
creates refraction of the light. Normally we don't want flare because it's
a kind of technical fault. But sometimes we like flare because it creates
something. The day before yesterday we shot a scene outside when the
boys are getting into [a house] and we did one shot with no flare and then
one with. It's one of those things we can't control. Sometimes it's a mistake, a happy accident.

**SH&LZ:** *Fans certainly appreciate the way Serge lights* Supernatural's
*lead actors.*

**Serge:** They're very handsome guys and they are easy to light because
they can take many kinds of lights and still look good. I can lay lights on
them, or if I want them to be dark and just have room light or a bit of
sidelight, I can do it. It's [because of] the structure of the face, the eyes.
Sometimes if you have an actor and the eyes are recessed, you have to
light in a certain way because otherwise you create a big shadow on their
face. But in a way, sometimes, not that I do that all the time, but I would
light them [Jared and Jensen] as I would light women. It's not to make a
gender separation, but there are some lighting that I would not use on a
woman that I would use on these guys – harder light, shadow across their
face – I would do exactly the same on a woman and it would not look good.
But them, they can take most lighting [...] Jared and Jensen influence the
look of the show in a way because they are so good technically that I can
have them perform little adjustments in their acting so they would catch
for instance that little ray of light that I want them to catch as they step
into a dark corner. That helps me a lot to keep the show on the dark side.
By being as good as they are, they provide me with that extra edge.

Images do have a subtext: what the image means before a single
word is spoken. On the one hand, something is shown; on the other hand,
something is said. Sometimes these two levels of meaning overlap, and
sometimes they contradict each other. It's a kind of semiotic game, and
I love being a part of it. Of course, the director is in charge of the game.
But these issues must be addressed, otherwise we only shoot what is obvious. Cinematography is not just about lighting. Light helps to create
meaning. A good script focuses on an essential conflict. As a cinematog-

rapher, I am looking for the essential light that will be the extension of that conflict and that will enable the viewer to experience it.

It takes a solid organization to synchronize fifty, sixty people. Organically, as a crew, we've been working for years now and we're still there, because we enjoy each other. Also the chemistry between the people is good. Sometimes you do a project, you're happy to end it after two weeks. [...] I think it's one of the reasons for the success of the show. It's the combination of all the creativity of everyone on the set toward the same goal.

**SH&LZ:** *The* Supernatural *cast and crew seem to see the fans as collaborators as well, and fans' creative input as part of the process.*

**Serge:** Over the years I've been going to websites where the fans express themselves. I found the quality of the sites I read are very good. Sometimes the analysis goes way beyond what you would expect. So I like the feedback, though I never interact with them. I like to go to the sites to keep in tune, keep informed, because it's for them that we do this. ●

### Acknowledgements
Screencaps compiled by Ash48 (Sarah House). All screencaps from *Home of the Nutty.com*. Additional contributors: el1ie, galwithglasses and missyjack

**Fan Appreciation no.2**
Serge Ladouceur: The Cinematographer

~~~~~~~~~~~~

**GO FURTHER**

**Film/Television**

'All Dogs Go to Heaven', Phil Sgriccia, dir. *Supernatural*
(Los Angeles: Warner Brothers, 2010)

'After School Special', Adam Kane, dir. *Supernatural* (Los Angeles: Warner Brothers, 2009)

'No Rest for the Wicked', Kim Manners, dir. *Supernatural*,
(Los Angeles: Warner Brothers, 2008)

*X-Files*, Chris Carter, creator (Los Angeles: 20th Century Fox Television 1993-2003)

'Lazarus Rising', Kim Manners, dir. *Supernatural* (Los Angeles: Warner Brothers, 2008)

'Scarecrow', Kim Manners dir. *Supernatural* (Los Angeles: Warner Brothers, 2006)

'When the Levee Breaks', Robert Singer, dir. *Supernatural*
(Los Angeles: Warner Brothers, 2009)

'Good God, Y'All', Philip Sgriccia, dir. *Supernatural* (Los Angeles: Warner Brothers, 2009).

'Clap Your Hands If You Believe', (John Showalter, dir. *Supernatural* (Los Angeles: Warner
Brothers, 2010)
'Jump The Shark', Phil Sgriccia, dir. *Supernatural* (Los Angeles: Warner Brothers, 2009)

'Swan Song', Steve Boyum, dir. *Supernatural* (Los Angeles: Warner Brothers, 2010)

'A Little Slice of Kevin', Charlie Carner, dir. *Supernatural*
(Los Angeles: Warner Brothers, 2012)

'What's Up, Tiger Mommy?', John Showalter, dir. *Supernatural*
(Los Angeles: Warner Brothers, 2012)

'Heartache', Jensen Ackles, dir. *Supernatural* (Los Angeles: Warner Brothers, 2012)

'The Born Again Identity', Robert Singer, dir. *Supernatural*
(Los Angeles: Warner Brothers, 2012)

'Hello Cruel World', Guy Bee, dir. *Supernatural* (Los Angeles: Warner Brothers, 2011)

'The End', Steve Boyum, dir. *Supernatural* (Los Angeles: Warner Brothers, 2009)

'The Song Remains The Same', Steve Boyum, dir. *Supernatural*
(Los Angeles: Warner Brothers, 2010)

'It's a Terrible Life', James L. Conway, dir. *Supernatural*
(Los Angeles: Warner Brothers, 2009)

'A Very Supernatural Christmas', J. Miller Tobin, dir. *Supernatural*
(Los Angeles: Warner Brothers, 2007)

'Bad Day at Black Rock', Robert Singer, dir. *Supernatural*
(Los Angeles: Warner Brothers, 2007)

'The Man Who Knew Too Much', Robert Singer, dir. *Supernatural*
(Los Angeles: Warner Brothers, 2011)

'Sympathy for the Devil', Robert Singer, dir. *Supernatural*
(Los Angeles: Warner Brothers, 2009)

'Heart', Kim Manners dir. *Supernatural* (Los Angeles Warner Brothers, 2007)

'Bloodlust', Robert Singer, dir. *Supernatural* (Los Angeles: Warner Brothers, 2006)

Chapter
8

# The Pro of Cons

Richard Speight, Jr.

→ When I entered the coffee shop I'm now sitting in, a woman at a table looked up from her book, gave me the once-over, then went back her reading, unimpressed. Earlier this morning, when I went to a café for breakfast, no heads turned. The other night, when I slipped inside a packed bar, absolutely no one was shocked and excited to see me.

*Figure 1: Richard and Fans, Chicago 2008. (photo by Lizz Sisson)*

There's a good reason for all these nonplussed reactions to my comings and goings – I'm not famous. No one stops me in the streets, has heart palpitations when I pass by, or interrupts my 'me' time with autograph requests. And yet for the past four years, somewhere between five and fifteen times a year, I make grown women shake and young girls *squee* (and maybe a couple of guys get sweaty palms). Why? Because I'm a regular guest at conventions for the CW show *Supernatural*. Am I one of the show's stars? Nope. A strong supporting character? Not even close. I appeared in a measly four episodes, playing first The Trickster who (spoiler alert!) later revealed himself to be the Archangel Gabriel. Four, total. On a show that has clocked over a hundred episodes and counting. Yet according to the web, I've so far been a featured guest at 33 conventions. That's an unbalanced ratio that leads to an obvious question – *Why*?

Let me clarify something – when I say 'convention', I don't mean a giant hall filled with displays promoting goods and services to the interested masses. I'm referring to the travelling roadshows that take lead actors, supporting characters and bit players from a TV show or film from town to town to meet their fan base face to face. For a fee, fans in North America, Europe, South America, Australia, and beyond can see people from their favourite shows live and in the flesh. Listen with glee as they tell droll stories of behind-the-scene antics. Join them for coffee. Even get their photo with them. I've been an actor my whole adult life, yet barring the Trekkie cliché that's been beaten to death for the last thirty years, I didn't know conventions for shows and movies even existed, which is why when I was first invited to appear at a *Supernatural* convention, I refused. I thought it was some sort of scam. It didn't make any sense to me that anyone would want to see or meet me after doing a whopping two episodes (at that time) of the show. Soon, another invitation came through. This time, my agent encouraged me to go. 'Meet some fans, make a few bucks … What could it hurt?' was her argument. Easy for her to say from her cushy office. I was the one heading off into the great unknown. But fine. I'm a team player. As ludicrous as the whole thing seemed to me, I bit the bullet and said yes.

It was Chicago, 2008. I was a 'con virgin' as people new to the circuit are called, and I was a panicky mess. When I arrived at the convention hotel, I immediately felt the eyes of people on me. Watching me. Whispering. A very weird sensation for a guy who, between guest spots, series regular roles, film parts and commercials, had been on-screen easily over a hundred of times, yet still moved through the universe undetected. But not here, not now. Not in this convention hotel in Chicago in 2008. I specifically remember

**The Pro of Cons**
Richard Speight, Jr.

the first two people *by name* who approached me to get a photograph in that lobby. It was a surreal experience.

First thing I noticed that really threw me: the fans were almost all women. No fat guys in Star Fleet uniforms. Women. There goes myth #1. The second thing I figured out over the course of that weekend: the fans weren't scary, creepy, socially inept or dangerous. (Or men.) Adios, myth #2. I was in a hotel full of women who were, for the most part, thrilled to have me there and excited to meet me. Strange. Bizarre. Fan- f*cking-tastic. The exact opposite of high school. They embraced me (sometimes literally), so I embraced them back. As I worked my way through the weekend, talking to people, signing their stuff, posing for their pictures, I got consistent feedback – 'My God, you're so normal!' Again, the exact opposite of high school. But the comment struck me. Why *wouldn't* I be normal? I suppose there are those actors who inflate their own sense of self-importance (or have it professionally inflated for them by one of Hollywood's top firms) and in so doing create a false separation between themselves and those who are paying to meet them. That's good, old-fashioned B.S. I act for a living. You're a teacher. Or a doctor. Or a yoga instructor. Or you're active military. There is nothing actors do that is more impressive or important than what anyone else does. In fact, nine times out of ten, the other professions represented at any given convention have far greater impact and social importance than what we're getting paid to do.

On the other hand, sometimes an actor's stand-offish behaviour is born from a real issue. They're shy. That's legit. I've seen it. It can be a very overwhelming experience, glad-handing that many people face to face. When you set out to be a performer, pressing the flesh is not in the job description. Not everyone is comfortable with it. I, however, am. Throwing me onstage with a mic is tantamount to tossing Br'er Rabbit into the briar patch. In that giant hall in front of those giddy women (and handful of men), I'm at home and in my element. I'm not sure why, but I dig it.

For actors, these weekends are very structured. Rules are in place and itineraries laid out so we know exactly what we will be doing and for how long. Convention-goers adhere to an even more rigid outline. They're handed a schedule and a seat number and ne'er do they deviate from what is printed on those precious pages. That is until I decided to shake things up. That's right, I'm talking about ... *Karaoke*!

Let me get a few things off my chest before I dive in. Traditional karaoke is my nemesis. I hate it. Especially the way it used to be done at all the North American *Supernatural* conventions (all thrown by the wonderful folks at Creation Entertainment). Again, I reference Chicago, 2008. One of my assignments was to attend the Friday night karaoke party – a definite misuse of the term 'party'. I know. I was there. Had to be. It was in my contract. It took place in the hotel lounge. Fans filled the tiny bar where, with the help of a generic karaoke DJ, they belted ballads to an audience of fellow fans waiting for the handful of guest actors to show up along with a few poor businessmen trying to down a beer and a bite after a long day of pedalling their wares around the Windy City. I went

Figure 2: Before the Karaoke Revolution. (photo courtesy of Richard Speight, Jr.)

in, convention rep in tow, spent my required 30 minutes explaining to every single person why I wasn't allowed to sign anything or take any pictures, then left as fast as humanly possible. It was socially awkward and claustrophobic. But it was a trip to the flippin' beach compared to the karaoke party's next incarnation.

I don't remember which city was next – all convention hotels start to feel the same after a while. I think it was either Vancouver or New Jersey. The itinerary came out – I was once again assigned to attend the karaoke party. But this time, it wasn't in the hotel bar, it was in the main hall. And we weren't going to mix and mingle in the crowd – we (the other actors with me were Aldis Hodge and Katherine Boecher) were going to be onstage, co-hosting the damn thing! So there we were, front and centre, with a smattering of fans waiting patiently for their song to be called. I say smattering because since the karaoke party was notoriously lame, hardly anyone was there, but those who *were* there were still in their assigned seats. Random heads dotting row after row of empty chairs. The huge hall had the sad, empty feel of a porno theatre on Easter Sunday and the freewheeling energy of the DMV waiting room.

Aldis, Katherine and I did our best to save face, re-enacting the lyrics to each song with high drama to try and hopefully draw a laugh or two. I specifically remember Katherine crawling around onstage, channeling her inner feline as someone sang 'Eye of the Tiger.' That was the high point of the night for me – that woman makes a helluva jungle cat. But despite our best stage antics, the evening still seemed bizarrely stilted. At the end of the event, I stepped off stage feeling like a complete a-hole. I felt bad for the people attending. If we were that miserable, it seemed almost impossible to me that they had much fun either.

Next city, same crappy assignment. Same agonizing knot in the pit of my stomach. This again? This 'talent show from hell' format? I couldn't do it. Not again. Backstage, I turned to Matt Cohen, one of the other actors about to join me onstage for this hideous cluster-f.

'This is going to suck.'
Matt, ever the upbeat chap, responded cheerily, 'No it won't. It'll be fun!'
'No it won't! It'll blow and we'll look like buttholes! I've done this before! It's a train wreck! It sucks!'
'So let's un-suck it.'

Brilliant, Matt. *Brilliant*! Let's un-suck it! Moments later, when we all took the stage, I grabbed the mic and said, 'I know that Creation's rules say you gotta stay in your assigned seat, but I say, "F*ck the rules!" This is our show and we want you all front and centre – right now!'

**The Pro of Cons**
Richard Speight, Jr.

Figure 3: After the Karaoke Revolution. (photo by Karen Cooke)

The fans in attendance exchanged glances – *Can we really do this? Will they throw us out?* Matt got the ball rolling by jumping off the stage and using his rippling torso to move chairs out of the way to create space up front. After a moment or two, the fans came down. Timidly, but they came. And suddenly, subtly, the change began. The energy was different. It was more relaxed. People sang. People cheered. People danced. *We* danced. The separation between actor and fan began to dissipate. And afterwards, people talked and tweeted and told others about what happened that night. And word began to spread.

Next city, Stephanie Dizon, Creation's kick-ass boots-on-the-ground operations manager at all our shows, pulled me aside. She appreciated what we'd done in (whatever city that was), but went on to explain Creation's position. People pay different amounts to sit in different sections, she reminded me, and the people up front who paid *beaucoup* bucks get annoyed if they feel they aren't getting what they paid for. She had to insist that I not tell fans to leave their assigned seats again. I listened. I nodded. I understood. I then hit the stage with Matt and grabbed the mic. 'F*ck the rules! No assigned seats! Everyone down front!'

The ladies – there in larger numbers than before – screamed with delight and bolted for the stage as if primed and ready for the command. I glanced at Steph. She shook her head and buried her face in her hands. But she was smiling. She got it. I *knew* she got it. And she knew I knew. And Matt knew that I knew she knew. The metamorphosis was complete. Matt and I had pulled it off. We weren't going to be able to put the toothpaste back in the tube. Moreover, we weren't even going to try. The karaoke party no longer sucked. It *rocked*. And beginning that night, it rocked with Creation's blessing.

Each successive party got bigger and better. The crowd doubled, then tripled. We didn't have to stack chairs anymore – Creation began setting up the room to accommodate the swelling numbers. Actors who weren't required to show up would come and stay all night. The backstage area took on the booze and food-fuelled atmosphere of a concert dressing room.

Then came the costumes.

This idea was born out of a meeting I called with Stephanie and Creation's head honchos, Adam Malin and Gary Berman. We all knew the karaoke party had become something special. It was time take it up a notch. Matt and I wanted to do T-shirts. Done. We wanted the night officially branded with our names. Handled. The Dick & Matt Karaoke Experience was born. Adam then threw out the idea of costumes. I loved it. It would

Figure 4: Richard Dresses the
Part. (photo by Karen Cooke)

humanize us by making us look like goofballs, and give our audience added incentive to get excited and get involved with their own crazy outfits. It was the polyester icing on an already swingin' cake. The Friday night event was no longer a time-killer in a hotel bar, it was a launch party for the entire weekend – and completely unique to the *Supernatural* cons. It let people know in no uncertain terms that this wasn't just another stodgy, formulaic convention. It was a *ride* – and everyone, actors included, were on board and ready to have a blast.

Why did changing the karaoke format have such an effect on people? Why did they respond so intensely and positively? In my opinion, when Matt and I broke down the performer/audience 'barrier' and insisted everyone get involved at the same level, we at the same time elevated the fans from observers to participants. They were no longer sitting in their seats watching the show – they *were* the show. And a direct correlation evolved between their commitment to the concept and the success of the party. They had *control*. If they wanted the night to rock, they now had the power to make it so with their passion and imagination. And this power ignited a fire in the fandom. True, we kicked opened the door, but they ran through it. They *stampeded* through it. And once they'd been on our side of the velvet rope (so to speak), there was no way they were going back. They were staying – and inviting their friends to join the fun.

Since Matt and I have now been dubbed the official Kings of Karaoke (in the *Supernatural* universe at least) let me offer some unsolicited advice. Call it a karaoke survival guide. Point #1: singing karaoke, like getting a driver's licence or wearing open-toed shoes, is a privilege, not a right. If you're tone-deaf – and I don't mean you can't

## The Pro of Cons
Richard Speight, Jr.

Figure 5: Actor Mark
Pellegrino Prepares to
Karaoke Crowd Surf.
(photo by Karen Cooke)

sing, I mean you have a voice so shrill and off-key it peels paint off the wall – maybe the karaoke stage isn't the place for you. Come! Show up! Be in the audience and sing along to your heart's content. Just show a little courtesy to the other eardrums in the room and avoid broadcasting your shrieks via microphone. Point #2: if the joint is jumping, don't bring it to a screeching halt with a love ballad. I don't care how moving your rendition of Bette Midler's 'The Rose' is, if you sing that right after someone just nailed 'Carry On, My Wayward Son', you, my friend, are now officially the brakeman on the train of fun. Point #3: for Pete's sake, don't sign up for a song you don't know. If you've never heard it and/or never sung it before – not even to yourself in the shower – onstage in front of a packed crowd probably isn't the best place to give it a shot. Remember – smartphones plus YouTube means, like it or not, your performance is going to live in perpetuity on the web. So do your homework, or in thirty years you'll have a tough time explaining to your grandkids why there's an Internet video of you warbling your way through 'My Heart Will Go On' in the key of M#.

Chicago, 2008 was four years ago. Almost five. I'm a long way from being a con virgin. I'm a seasoned veteran, the crusty old colonel who's been in the field for years and has seen hell rain down from the skies and has lived to tell the tale. OK, that's a bit extreme, but let's face it, I've been doing this a while. A fan recently tweeted that she was annoyed at her boyfriend or dad or whomever for giving her a hard time about going to *Supernatural* conventions and hanging out with 'C-level actors'. She found the classification offensive. And since those words were describing me as well as some of my pals, maybe I should have been offended, too. But I wasn't. I got a good laugh out of the whole

Figure 6: Actor Rob Benedict breaks down the barriers at Karaoke. (photo by Christopher Schmelke)

thing. Like I said, I know I'm not famous. I wait in lines and pay for my own clothes and fly coach. Who cares? I love what I do. I dreamt of being an actor my entire childhood, and now I'm living the dream, so to speak. Once, in reference to the perennial ups and downs of the entertainment business, *Supernatural* executive producer Bob Singer quipped, 'It ain't all blow-jobs and Jacuzzis.' So true. But even on its worst day, it's a damn cool way to make a living.

*Supernatural* is blessed to have so many passionate fans willing to spend their hard-earned dollars to travel Lord knows how many miles to hang out with us for a weekend. So every so often, I pack my bag, leave my real life, show up at a hotel and check in under my alias (that's Creation's rule. I don't really think it's necessary, but I suppose it adds to the mystique. I just wish they'd let me pick my own name. I'm dying to ask a buttoned-up hotel clerk to find a room with a view for 'Pat McCrotch'). The point is it seems that, at least for now, I'm a regular fixture on the *Supernatural* Dog n' Pony show, there to help deliver the experience the fans are hoping to have. I'm the approachable actor, the Karaoke King, the funny front man, the silly sidekick. And to many of them, I am, for lack of a better word, famous. Who am I to tell them they're wrong? They're having fun, I'm having fun. No one is getting hurt (unless there's another outbreak of karaoke stage-diving or Matt hurls another chair). I just show up and play the part I'm expected to play. Is that weird? Perhaps. But at its core, it's still just acting. It's what I do. So maybe sometimes, instead of on a stage or on a set, I do it in a convention hall. And maybe somehow, in some people's eyes, that makes me C level. But if it all translates to four years and 33-plus cons and thousands upon thousands of happy fans, then I think C is a pretty sweet level to be on.

As long as Mr McCrotch gets that room with a view. ●

# Contributor Details

### EDITORS

**Lynn Zubernis** is a clinical psychologist and Associate Professor at West Chester University of Pennsylvania. She is the area chair for Stardom and Fandom of the Southwest Popular Culture Association, and the Associate Editor of the *Journal of Fandom Studies*. Lynn is also an avid *Supernatural* fan. Together with Katherine Larsen, she has authored *Fangasm: Supernatural Fangirls* (2013) and *Fandom At The Crossroads: Celebration, Shame and Fan/Producer Relationships (2012)*, and edited *Fan Culture: Theory/Practice* (2012)

**Katherine Larsen** is an Assistant Teaching Professor at The George Washington University. She is co-author, with Lynn Zubernis, of *Fandom at the Crossroads: Celebration, Shame and Fan Producer Relationships* (2012) and *Fangasm: Supernatural Fangirls* (2013) and co-editor of *Fan Culture: Theory/Practice* (2012). She serves as the area chair for Fan Culture and Theory for both the Popular Culture Association and POPCANZ (the Popular Culture Association of Australia and New Zealand) and is the Principal Editor of the *Journal of Fandom Studies*.

### CONTRIBUTORS

**Paul Booth** is an assistant professor at DePaul University. He is the author of *Digital Fandom: New Media Studies* (Peter Lang, 2010) and *Time on TV: Temporal Displacement and Mashup Television* (Peter Lang, 2012), and the editor of *Fan Phenomena: Doctor Who* (Intellect, 2013). He is currently enjoying a cup of coffee.

**Mary Frances Casper**, MSPR, PhD is an Associate Professor in the Department of Communication at Boise State University. Casper has been at Boise State University since fall 2006 where she serves as the Public Relations Certificate Program Director and teaches public relations, media studies, and visual communication courses. Her scholarship shares the same underlying questions: What role do media messages play in our understandings of reality and the world, our expectations of the good life, and our concepts of self and identity? Her interest lies primarily with gender and groups often marginalized by media: women, children, and those considered Other. Recent work explores fan culture, community, and identification. Casper resides in Boise, Idaho with her husband, five children, three dogs, cat, fish, and hedgehog. She is a visual artist and admitted pop culture junkie, and is thrilled to have a career that requires her to watch television, peruse You Tube, scour social media, and wallow through the Web.

**Misha Collins** stars as Castiel in The CW's thriller *Supernatural*. Collins was born in Boston, Massachusetts. Before turning to acting, he worked as an intern at the White House during the Clinton Administration in the Office of Presidential Personnel. He then worked for National Public Radio on a show called *Weekly Edition*. In addition to his role on *Supernatural*, Collins' other television appearances include recurring roles on *ER* and *24* and guest appearances on *Nip/Tuck, CSI:NY, NCIS, Monk, Close to Home* and *NYPD Blue*. On the big screen, Collins is best known for his role as serial killer Paul Bernardo in the film *Karla*. Other film credits include *Par 6, Moving Alan, Liberty Heights, Girl Interrupted* and *Stonehenge Apocalypse*. In addition, Collins is a published poet with works in *The Columbia Poetry Review, The California Quarterly* and other literary journals. Collins currently resides in Los Angeles, enjoys endurance sports and has completed ultra-marathons.

**Mary F. Dominiak**, online as Bardicvoice, has been a *Supernatural* fan from the beginning of the series, and began writing episode commentaries and meta essays during the second season. A lawyer by training, Mary spent 22.5 years doing chemical risk management and risk communication work for the U.S. Environmental Protection Agency. She recently started her own voiceover business, BardicVoice Studio, recording audiobooks and e-learning courses. She took her J.D. from Georgetown University Law Center in 1979, and received her B.A./Honors undergraduate degree from the University of Wisconsin/Milwaukee in 1976. Mary's *Supernatural* essays can be found at http://bardicvoice.livejournal.com/.

**Sarah House (Ash48)** lives in Perth, Western Australia with her husband and teenage daughter. She's a primary school teacher who specialises in Drama and Media Arts. In 2005 she discovered a television show that captured her heart and mind. In 2006 she joined the many fans sharing their love of the show on-line. In late 2006 she decided to try her hand at making a fanvid. She discovered the process is very enjoyable (and addictive) and it soon occupied much of her free time. She also enjoys acting and spends what is left of her free time involved with the local theatre group.

**Bridget Kies** researches masculinity on television and in fan practices. Long before *Supernatural* premiered, she was an avid classic rock fan. She currently lives in Milwaukee, where she teaches courses on film and television. She is lucky to have a job where listening to AC/DC and watching TV count as "research." Her Twitter handle is @BridgetKies.

**Serge Ladouceur** is the Director of Photography for the television show *Supernatural*. He spent four years working for the Canadian Broadcasting Corporation as a camera assistant before studying at the London International Film School. Serge's influences include the film-noir aesthetic and the French New Wave (Nouvelle Vague) with its free form and spontaneous camera work. Serge enjoys the horror/fantasy genre both as a spectator and as a filmmaker. He enjoys creating atmosphere for the audience, and looks at cinematography as not just about lighting, but using light to create meaning.

**Lisa Macklem**, BA, JD, LLM, is currently pursuing further studies at the University of Western Ontario in Media Studies, and is in her second year as a Grand NCE-funded HQP. She is on the editorial boards for *The Journal of International Media and Entertainment Law* and *The Journal of Fan Studies*. She has published on fan fiction, copyright law, and jurisprudence and has presented numerous papers on *Supernatural*. Grand NCE has provided invaluable support for her continuing research.

As an actor, **Richard Speight, Jr.** starred in the award winning HBO mini-series *Band of Brothers*, the CBS series *The Agency*, and *Into The West* for TNT; has had recurring roles on *Justified*, *Supernatural*, *Look* for Showtime, and the cult hit *Jericho*; has made guest appearances on numerous shows including *Longmire*, *Memphis Beat*, *Life*, *ER*, *Alias*, *CSI: Miami*, and *Yes, Dear*; and has hawked just about every product known to man in his over 60 national commercials. In addition, he co-wrote and starred in *Open Water 2: Adrift* for LionsGate Films, and wrote, directed, and produced the award winning short film *America 101*. Richard was born and raised in Nashville, Tennessee, is a *cum laude* graduate of the University of Southern California, is the father of three and the husband of one.

**Jules Wilkinson** was raised by television in the wilds of suburbia in Melbourne, Australia and is the same age as *Doctor Who*. A writer of original and fan fiction, she also takes to the stage doing stand-up. A fangirl to her core, Jules runs the Supernatural Wiki, which is a repository for everything about *Supernatural* and its fandom.

# <u>Image Credits</u>

**From *Supernatural* the series**

Chapter 1:   Figs. 1-6 pages 15-18
Chapter 2:   Figs. 1-6 pages 23-24 & 26-28
Chapter 3:   Figs. 1-11 pages 36-40 & 42
Chapter 5:   Fig. 1 p.60
             Fig. 2 p.63
Chapter 6:   Figs. 1-6 pages 69-72
Chapter 7:   Fig. 1 p.81
Chapter 9:   Figs. 1-20 pages 95-96, 98, 100-101, 103-104, 106-108, 110-113

**Additional Images**

Intro:       Fig. 1 p.6 @ Christopher Schmelke
             Fig. 2 p.8 @ Karen Cooke
Chapter 6:   Fig. 7 p.73 @ Mary Dominiak
Chapter 7:   Fig. 2 p.81 @ Christopher Schmelke
             Figs. 3-4 p.82 @ Karen Cooke
             Figs. 5-6 p.84 @ Misha Collins
Chapter 8:   Fig. 1 p.87 @ Lizz Sisson
             Fig. 2 p.89 @ Richard Speight Jr.
             Figs.3-5 pages 90-92 @ Karen Cooke
             Fig. 6 p.93 @ Christopher Shmelke
Chapter 9:   (interviewee photo) p. 95 @ Serge Ladouceur
Chapter 10:  Figs. 1-9, pages 120-122, 124-125, 129, 131-132 @ Sarah House
             (interviewee photo) p. 119 @ Stuart Ridgway

# 'HOUSE RULES, SAMMY. DRIVER PICKS THE MUSIC, SHOTGUN SHUTS HIS CAKEHOLE.'

**DEAN TO SAM IN 'PILOT'.**
SEASON 1, EPISODE 1

# FAN PHENOMENA

OTHER TITLES AVAILABLE IN THE SERIES

**Star Trek**
Edited by Bruce E. Drushel
ISBN: 978-1-78320-023-8
£15.50 / $22

**Star Wars**
Edited by Mika Elovaara
ISBN: 978-1-78320-022-1
£15.50 / $22

**The Big Lebowski**
Edited by Zachary Ingle
ISBN: 978-1-78320-202-7
£15.50 / $22

**Sherlock Holmes**
Edited by Tom Ue
and Jonathan Cranfield
ISBN: 978-1-78320-205-8
£15.50 / $22

**Doctor Who**
Edited by Paul Booth
ISBN: 978-1-78320-020-7
£15.50 / $22

**Buffy the Vampire Slayer**
Edited by Jennifer K. Stuller
ISBN: 978-1-78320-019-1
£15.50 / $22

**Twin Peaks**
Edited by Marisa C. Hayes
and Franck Boulegue
ISBN: 978-1-78320-024-5
£15.50 / $22

**Audrey Hepburn**
Edited by Jacqui Miller
ISBN: 978-1-78320-206-5
£15.50 / $22

For further information about the series
and news of forthcoming titles visit **www.intellectbooks.com**